SHAPE
------------ by ------------
SHAPE
COLLECTION 2

Free-Motion Quilting
with Angela Walters

70+ More Designs
for Blocks, Backgrounds
& Borders

stashBOOKS.
an imprint of C&T Publishing

Text copyright © 2016 by Angela Walters

Photography and artwork copyright © 2016 by C&T Publishing, Inc.

Publisher: Amy Marson

Creative Director: Gailen Runge

Editors: Liz Aneloski and Karla Menaugh

Technical Editor: Priscilla Read

Cover/Book Designer: April Mostek

Production Coordinator: Zinnia Heinzmann

Production Editors: Jessica Brotman and Jennifer Warren

Illustrator: Eric Sears

Photo Assistant: Sarah Frost

Instructional photography by Diane Pedersen, unless otherwise noted

Published by Stash Books, an imprint of C&T Publishing, Inc., P.O. Box 1456, Lafayette, CA 94549

Library of Congress Cataloging-in-Publication Data

Names: Walters, Angela, 1979- author.

Title: Free-motion quilting with Angela Walters. 70+ more designs for blocks, backgrounds & borders / Angela Walters.

Description: Lafayette, CA : Stash Books, an imprint of C&T Publishing, Inc., [2016] | Series: Shape by shape ; collection 2 | Includes index.

Identifiers: LCCN 2015039095 | ISBN 9781617451829 (soft cover)

Subjects: LCSH: Patchwork quilts. | Patchwork--Patterns. | Quilting--Patterns. | Quilting--Design.

Classification: LCC TT835 .W356529 2016 | DDC 746.46--dc23

LC record available at http://lccn.loc.gov/2015039095

Printed in the USA

10 9 8 7 6 5

CONTENTS

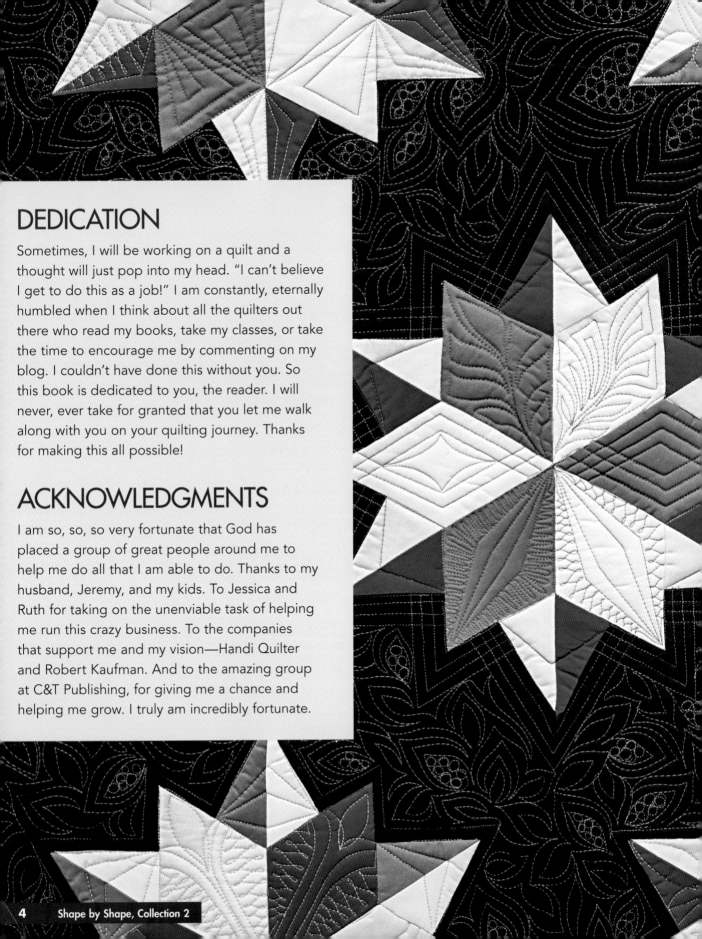

DEDICATION

Sometimes, I will be working on a quilt and a thought will just pop into my head. "I can't believe I get to do this as a job!" I am constantly, eternally humbled when I think about all the quilters out there who read my books, take my classes, or take the time to encourage me by commenting on my blog. I couldn't have done this without you. So this book is dedicated to you, the reader. I will never, ever take for granted that you let me walk along with you on your quilting journey. Thanks for making this all possible!

ACKNOWLEDGMENTS

I am so, so, so very fortunate that God has placed a group of great people around me to help me do all that I am able to do. Thanks to my husband, Jeremy, and my kids. To Jessica and Ruth for taking on the unenviable task of helping me run this crazy business. To the companies that support me and my vision—Handi Quilter and Robert Kaufman. And to the amazing group at C&T Publishing, for giving me a chance and helping me grow. I truly am incredibly fortunate.

INDEX
OF QUILTING DESIGNS

SQUARES and RECTANGLES

Square 1
(page 20)

Square 2
(page 22)

Square 3
(page 24)

Square 4
(page 25)

Square 5
(page 26)

Square 6
(page 28)

Square 7
(page 29)

Square 8
(page 30)

Square 9
(page 31)

Square 10
(page 32)

TRIANGLES

Triangle 1
(page 36)

Triangle 2
(page 37)

Triangle 3
(page 38)

Triangle 4
(page 39)

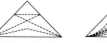

Triangle 5
(page 40)

Triangle 6
(page 41)

Triangle 7
(page 42)

Triangle 8
(page 43)

Triangle 9
(page 44)

Triangle 10
(page 45)

CIRCLES

Circle 1
(page 48)

Circle 2
(page 49)

Circle 3
(page 50)

Circle 4
(page 51)

Circle 5
(page 52)

Circle 6
(page 53)

Circle 7
(page 54)

Circle 8
(page 55)

Circle 9
(page 56)

Circle 10
(page 57)

DIAMONDS

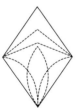
Diamond 1
(page 60)

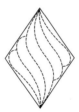
Diamond 2
(page 61)

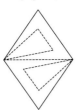
Diamond 3
(page 62)

Diamond 4
(page 63)

Diamond 5
(page 64)

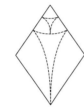
Diamond 6
(page 65)

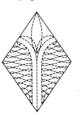
Diamond 7
(page 66)

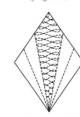
Diamond 8
(page 67)

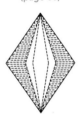
Diamond 9
(page 68)

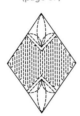
Diamond 10
(page 69)

HEXAGONS

Hexagon 1
(page 72)

Hexagon 2
(page 73)

Hexagon 3
(page 74)

Hexagon 4
(page 75)

Hexagon 5
(page 76)

Hexagon 6
(page 77)

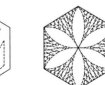
Hexagon 7
(page 78)

Hexagon 8
(page 79)

Hexagon 9
(page 80)

Hexagon 10
(page 81)

BACKGROUND FILLERS

Starburst
(page 86)

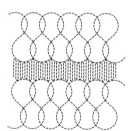

Ribbon Rows
(page 88)

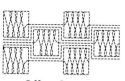

Offset Squares
(page 90)

Pebbled Leaves
(page 92)

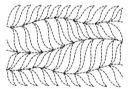

Wavy Serpentine Lines
(page 94)

Woven Arcs
(page 96)

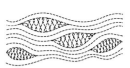

Woodgrain Variation
(page 98)

Echoed Pebbles
(page 100)

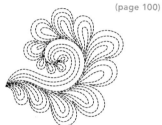

Paisley Feather
(page 102)

BORDERS

Tiered Lines
(page 108)

Serpentine Clusters
(page 110)

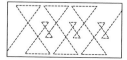

Big and Little Zigzags
(page 112)

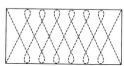

Double Wishbones
(page 114)

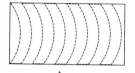

Arcs
(page 116)

Nested Swirls
(page 118)

Triangle Wedges
(page 120)

Angled Lines
(page 122)

Swirl Hook Chain
(page 124)

INTRODUCTION

Sometimes I think that I would like to make an infomercial about the tragedy of unquilted quilt tops. It would, of course, star a quilt top, stuck in a drawer and never allowed to serve its purpose. Sad music would be playing in the background, which would bring tears to your eyes. Then, since I am making this all up in my head anyway, Morgan Freeman's voice would narrate the commercial, saying something like, "Every year, hundreds of quilts aren't finished. Instead, they are left alone and put aside. What can you do to help this tragedy?"

Okay, so that's a little dramatic, but it's true. So many quilters make a quilt top and put it aside, thinking they will wait until they are "good enough" at quilting to quilt it. Or perhaps they are unsure of what designs to use, so they wait until the perfect idea strikes them. But I always say, "A finished quilt is better than a perfect quilt top." Your quilts can't serve their purpose if you aren't finishing them!

That is the reason I love to write books, especially this one! I want to encourage you to finish your quilts and help make selecting quilting designs a little easier. Selecting designs can be as difficult as actually quilting … well, almost. So the next time you get stuck, pull out this book as a reference.

I can't count the number of times that I have looked at a quilt and forgotten every quilting design that I know. I have found that instead of being overwhelmed by the whole quilt, it's better to look at the individual components of the quilt. That's why this book will show you several different designs for all parts of a quilt. My hope is that you will learn some new designs and also will feel encouraged and ready to quilt your quilt top.

What About the Machine

I tend to do most of my quilting on a Handi Quilter longarm quilting machine, but all the designs in this book can be done on any kind of machine. That's why I show all the illustrations without showing the machine used. I don't want that to be a stumbling point for anyone reading this book. So no matter what kind of machine you use, what style of quilting you like, or even what type of thread you like best, these designs are just for you!

Ready?
Now, let's get to the fun part: the quilting!

section 1:
QUILT BLOCKS

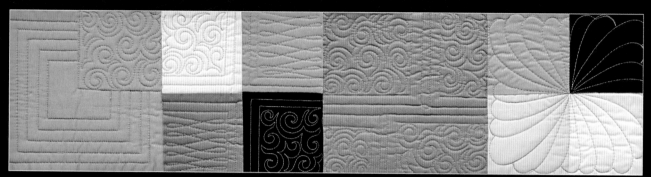

SQUARES AND RECTANGLES 18

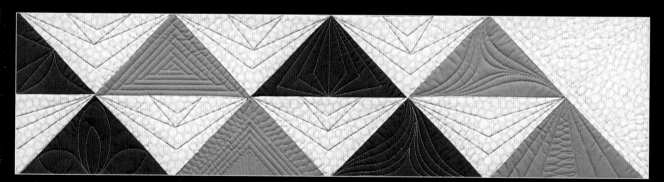

TRIANGLES 34

CIRCLES 46

This section focuses on quilt blocks with designs for basic shapes—squares, rectangles, triangles, circles, diamonds, and hexagons. Each chapter will show you several designs for that shape and variations of the designs, as well as tips for choosing the perfect area to put them on your quilts.

DIAMONDS 58

HEXAGONS 70

So Why the Shapes?

Choosing quilting designs for your quilt blocks can be a little overwhelming. But looking past the block as a whole and focusing on the different shapes that compose it can make the process a little easier. Some blocks are easier to "break down" than others, but most can be divided into basic shapes. Here are a few tips to make the process easier.

note To help illustrate my point, here are three quilts made from the same block. One is the unquilted version and the other two are quilted, each showing different quilting options.

Pieced by Ruth Doss

Pieced by Ruth Doss and quilted by Angela Walters

Pieced by Ruth Doss and quilted by Angela Walters

Breaking It Down

What else can you do besides look at the obvious shapes?

▶ COMBINE SIMILAR BLOCKS TO MAKE A LARGER BLOCK.

An easy solution is to combine smaller blocks to form bigger blocks. Not only will this possibly spark a design idea, but it might create secondary designs within your quilt.

A Nine-Patch block is a perfect example. Instead of quilting each block separately, you can quilt the larger square as a whole.

Or, combine three rectangles and quilt them as one larger square.

Quilted using a variation of Triangle 10 (page 45)

Square 7 quilting design (page 29)

▶ LOOK FOR THE HIDDEN.

Looking a little closer can reveal the hidden shapes in blocks as well. Try combining multiple parts of the blocks to make different shapes. This is especially great for dealing with smaller blocks, or if you have a piecing issue that you want to cover up!

For example, I quilted two triangles and a Nine-Patch block as a larger triangle block.

You can pick and choose which blocks you want to combine. In this Nine-Patch block, I combined some of the squares and quilted them so that they wrap around a bottom square.

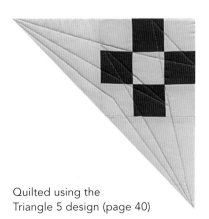

Quilted using the
Triangle 5 design (page 40)

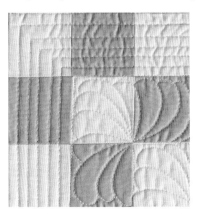

Using the quilting to create your own shapes works especially well for larger blocks, or when you want to add something different to the background areas of a quilt. Just quilt the shape of a block and quilt it as you would normally.

In fact, once you get into the book you may quickly notice that this is my favorite way of coming up with designs. The Triangle 9 design is an example. I used the quilting to create a hexagon in the middle and quilted it the same way I would quilt a hexagon quilt block.

In this example, I used the quilting to divide the square into four triangles and quilted them separately.

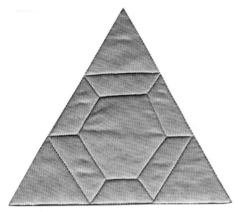

Triangle 9 (page 44)

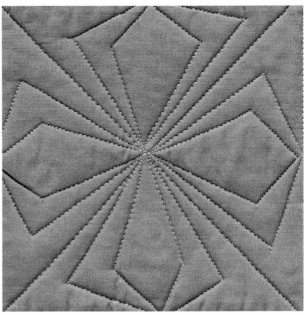

Triangle 2 (page 37)

This is great technique for those designs that you are anxious to try out!

More Help for Choosing Designs

Most designs can be easily be adapted for blocks of different shapes. On the example quilt, I used diamond designs in some of the half-square triangle blocks.

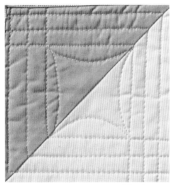

Diamond 5 in a square block (page 64)

Diamond 1 variation (page 60)

Diamond 3 variation (page 62)

In the example quilt, I used the Starburst background design (page 86) in the square blocks, rotating the direction of the lines so that they wrap around the block.

The Starburst design in the dark orange squares helps frame the center of the quilt.

Seeing Beyond the Basic Design

It is possible that you may not be crazy about one of the designs in this book. Instead of passing it over, use your imagination to see what you can do to make it fit your preferences.

Let's take Circle 5 (page 52) for example.

Circle 5

If you don't like the way it looks in a circle block, try it in a different shape, such as a hexagon.

Use a circle motif in a hexagon or another shape.

▶ DON'T FORGET ABOUT SECONDARY DESIGNS.

Some of the designs can make really interesting secondary patterns when used together, even if they seem basic at first glance.

Diamond 8 (page 67) is the perfect example. When used in a group of hexagons, it creates an intricate pattern.

Or, imagine it in a group of blocks.

Circle 5 in adjacent blocks

Also consider what a design might look like when combined with a variation in groups of blocks. This group of diamonds alternates between Diamond 9 and its variation (page 68).

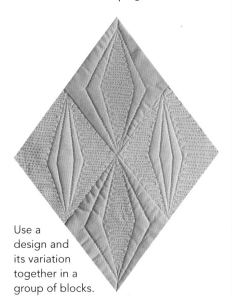

Use a design and its variation together in a group of blocks.

Diamond 8 creates a wonderful secondary design in a group of hexagons.

What about Other Shapes?

If you have pieced a block shape that isn't in the book, try looking at the quilting designs for a similar shape. For instance, tumbler blocks are similar to squares.

Tumbling block quilted with Square 3 design (page 24)

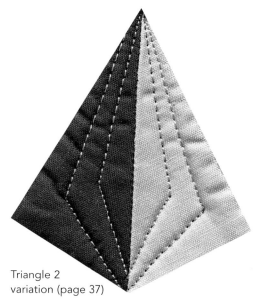

Triangle 2 variation (page 37)

Stitch a different border design in each wedge of a fan.

▶ SOME BORDER DESIGNS CAN WORK IN WEDGE-SHAPED BLOCKS.

If that doesn't work, find a design that you like and tweak it to fit. Try adding more echo lines or different fillers to adapt it to the shape.

Ready?

Let's get started with the designs!

SQUARES
AND RECTANGLES

Pieced by Ruth Doss and quilted by Angela Walters

The most basic of quilt block shapes is the square or rectangular block. Irish Chains, Nine-Patches, and Log Cabins are just a few examples. The designs in this section are some of my favorites for these blocks. I hope they will put you in a square frame of mind!

Other Ways to Use These Designs

All of these designs can be tweaked to create some fun variations. With these designs as starting points, use your imagination to see what you can come up with. Most of these designs can be used in blocks of other shapes, including hexagons and triangles.

Of course, not all quilts will have square or rectangular blocks. But if you look closely enough at your quilt tops, chances are that squares or rectangles might pop out at you in the least likely of places. You can combine blocks of different shapes to make squares. Or try one as a border treatment, because borders can be broken into repeating squares and rectangles.

Square 5 quilted as a border design

THIS DESIGN IS ALL ABOUT THE ECHOING, MAKING IT A REALLY FORGIVING DESIGN. WHEN IN DOUBT, JUST ADD MORE ECHO LINES. THE DENSE QUILTING IS PERFECT FOR DRAWING YOUR EYES TO THE BLOCKS YOU WANT TO HIGHLIGHT. IT DOESN'T MATTER IF YOU ARE QUILTING LARGER OR SMALLER BLOCKS; THIS DESIGN WORKS WELL IN BOTH.

SQUARE 1

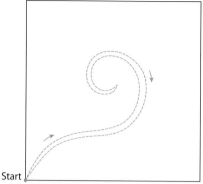

Start

1. Starting from any corner of the block, quilt an elongated swirl that ends toward the center of the block. Echo back to the starting point. I tend to make my swirls look like a question mark.

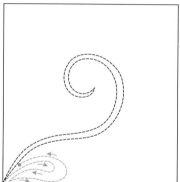

2. At the bottom of the swirl, quilt a paisley shape and echo around it once or twice.

TIP

To make the paisley petals fit the area, quilt them so that they are "merging" into the swirl.

3. Continue working your way around the swirl, quilting paisleys and echoing until you get to the center of the swirl.

4. Echo along the swirl, returning close to the starting point. This allows you to quickly and easily move on to the next block.

TIP

Remember, the answer is almost always echoing. If the design doesn't fill the area as much as you want or if you find yourself stuck, just echo around the petals.

VARIATION

Quilt the design in smaller blocks, rotating the placement, to create a repetitive look.

Try quilting the pattern in a set of adjacent blocks.

THIS DESIGN IS MY FAVORITE TYPE—IT LOOKS A LOT HARDER TO STITCH THAN IT ACTUALLY IS. IT DOESN'T REQUIRE ANY MARKING AND CAN HELP BREAK UP BIGGER SQUARE BLOCKS.

note When I quilt this on my longarm, I most likely will use a ruler. On a sewing machine, you can use a walking foot if you're working on a smaller project. If you use the free-motion quilting foot, don't stress too much about making the lines perfectly straight. Straightish is good enough!

SQUARE 2

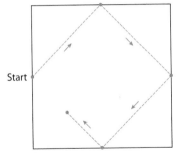

Start

1. Starting at the middle of a side, quilt a diagonal line to the halfway point of the next side. Continue working your way around the block, stopping halfway through the last line.

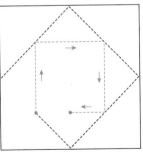

2. Quilt a line up to the halfway point of the first line you quilted, and continue quilting lines. Stop halfway through the last line.

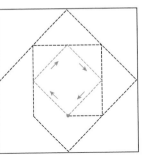

3. Repeat 1 more time, quilting a diamond shape and returning to the starting point.

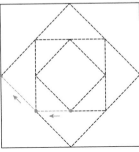

4. Work your way out of the center by quilting a horizontal line, then a diagonal line back to the original starting point.

note Don't worry if you aren't hitting the midpoint perfectly. Just use that as a reference point.

VARIATIONS

If this design seems a little too complex, try it in a Four-Patch block first. The seams give you the perfect starting points. I also added more lines to the design, an easy thing to do for larger blocks.

If you want denser quilting, or need to fill in space in larger blocks, fill in the corners with a different design. I especially like using curved lines.

To fill in a large block, add curved lines in the corners.

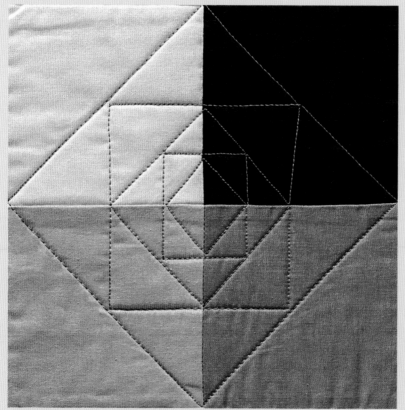

Use the seams of a Four-Patch block as reference points for this square-in-a-square design.

Diagonal lines also look great.

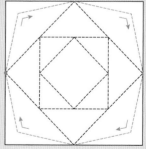

Diagonal lines also help fill in the corners.

Experiment to see how many other different variations you can come up with.

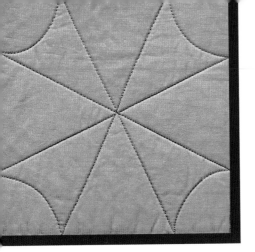

THIS DESIGN IS A PLAY ON THE CONTINUOUS CURVE DESIGN. IT'S A QUICK AND EASY DESIGN TO QUILT, AND THE VARIATIONS ARE ENDLESS. YOU WILL NEED TO DO A LITTLE TRAVELING ALONG THE EDGE OF THE BLOCK, BUT THE RESULT IS WELL WORTH IT!

VARIATIONS

For a more geometric look, use straight lines instead of curved lines.

Use straight lines instead of curves.

Try it in a Four-Patch block as a way to connect the squares. It's also helpful to have the corners as a reference.

Stitching this design over a Four-Patch block will pull the block together.

SQUARE 3

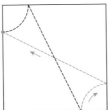

Start

1. Starting about 2″ away from any corner, quilt a curved line that ends about 2″ on the adjacent side. Quilt a diagonal line to approximately 2″ away from the opposite corner.

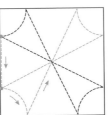

2. Quilt a curved line that ends about 2″ away from the new corner's adjacent side, then quilt a diagonal line that ends at the original starting point.

3. Travel along the edge of the block until you are about 2″ away from the next corner. Repeat Steps 1 and 2 to fill in the design in the remaining corners.

note I prefer traveling along the block edge to start the next shape because I can ensure that the lines cross in the center. If you prefer to omit the traveling, try this alternative option. Stitch from the first corner to the center of the block, then on to the next corner. A benefit of this technique is that it starts and ends at the same place.

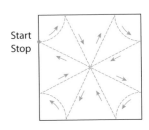

Start
Stop

SQUARE 4

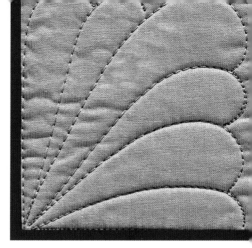

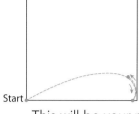

1. First, decide on a starting point. This will be your pivot corner, meaning that all of the lines will come back to this point. Quilt a softly curving line that makes a sharper curve toward the adjacent corner just before you reach the other side of the block. Travel back along the curve about ½˝.

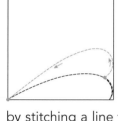

2. Quilt the next petal of the feather by stitching a line that curves out a bit and then returns to the starting corner.

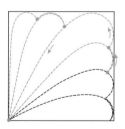

3. Continue quilting the petals, filling in the block as much as possible.

note The petal that goes to the opposite corner from the starting point will be bigger than the rest.

4. To move on to the next block, travel along the block edges.

THIS DESIGN FITS THE PETALS OF A FEATHER INTO A SQUARE SHAPE. I LIKE TO USE IT IN SMALLER SQUARES, ESPECIALLY ON IRISH CHAIN QUILTS, OR AS A WAY TO SOFTEN THE CORNERS OF A COMPLEX BLOCK. YOU CAN USE THIS BLOCK DESIGN AS A GREAT WAY TO PRACTICE FEATHER DESIGNS WITHOUT COMMITTING TO USING THEM OVER THE WHOLE QUILT.

VARIATION

Quilting 4 blocks with the same pivot point will give you a design that looks like a feather wreath but is much easier to quilt!

Create a wreath design by quilting 4 blocks with the same pivot point.

I KNOW THAT QUILTING DESIGNS ARE SUPPOSED TO BE LIKE MY KIDS—I SHOULDN'T HAVE FAVORITES. BUT RIGHT NOW, THIS ONE IS MY FAVORITE! IT'S BEST FOR RECTANGULAR BLOCKS, BUT I ALSO LOVE TO QUILT IT IN SASHING STRIPS OR TO LINK QUILT BLOCKS. IT REALLY ADDS A STRIKING SECONDARY PATTERN TO THE QUILTING.

SQUARE 5

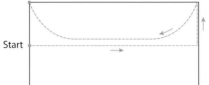

1. Start at the halfway point on the shortest side and quilt a horizontal line to the other side. Travel along the block edge and quilt a line that curves down, echoes the straight line, and curves back to the opposite corner.

note I quilt the horizontal line first to help ensure that the design looks symmetrical.

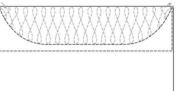

2. Fill the area above the curved line with the design of your choice. I like to use the wishbone design. Work your way across to the other side of the block.

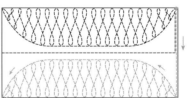

3. Travel along the edge of the block to the bottom corner. Stitch another curved line and filler to echo the top half of the block.

VARIATIONS

Instead of quilting a filler design, you could add a few echoed lines.

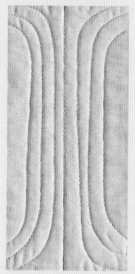

Add echoed lines for a different look.

Using this design in different layouts will really show off its versatility!

Use it in the background to connect 2 blocks.

Stretch the design over 2 or more blocks to tie them together.

Or quilt it in a continuous line for a funky border design.

Create an unusual sashing or border pattern by stitching the design in a continuous line.

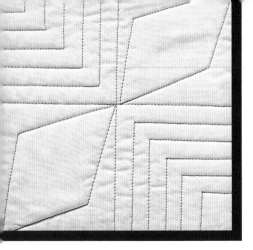

I LOVE DIVIDING BLOCKS INTO SMALLER SHAPES. THE SMALLER AREAS ARE A LITTLE EASIER TO STITCH, AND THE DIVISIONS CAN CREATE SOME SECONDARY DESIGNS THAT ARE REALLY BEAUTIFUL. THIS DESIGN IS BEST FOR MEDIUM TO LARGE BLOCKS AND CAN BE CHANGED EASILY FOR A VARIETY OF LOOKS.

VARIATION

Of course you can use different designs in each of the smaller squares, but you also can change up the design as it is. In this example, I added more echo lines inside the diamonds and varied the spacing between the echo lines.

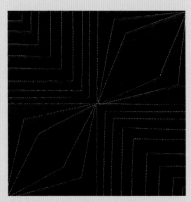

Add more lines and stagger the spacing for a different look.

SQUARE 6

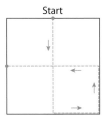

Start

1. Break the block into 4 smaller squares. Quilt a vertical line down the middle of the block. Travel along the edges to the midpoint of the adjacent side and quilt a horizontal line to the opposite side.

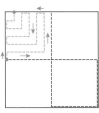

2. Fill in the top left square by echoing the quilting lines, traveling in between lines.

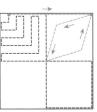

3. Travel along the top edge of the block to the next outer corner, and quilt a diamond-shaped design that touches the center of the block and returns to the starting point.

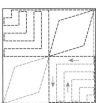

4. Travel along the edge of the block to repeat Steps 2 and 3 in the bottom half of the square.

SQUARE 7

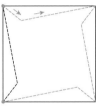

1. Starting from any corner of the block, quilt a short line that goes out at an angle and then changes direction to end at the next corner.

note Don't worry about the exact angle of the first line. Instead make sure that the line pivots, or changes direction, sooner rather than later.

2. Work your way around the block, repeating Step 1 from corner to corner.

3. You can stop at the end of Step 2 or echo inside the lines that you just quilted. The echoed lines will give the design a slightly different look.

WHAT HAPPENS WHEN YOU ARE INSPIRED BY A NINJA THROWING STAR? YOU GET THIS FUNKY, ANGULAR DESIGN THAT IS PERFECT FOR SMALLER SQUARES. THE BONUS IS THAT YOU END UP IN THE SAME PLACE THAT YOU START, MAKING IT EASY TO MOVE ON TO THE NEXT BLOCK WHEN YOU ARE FINISHED. NOW THAT'S QUICK AND EASY QUILTING!

VARIATION

This design starts and ends at the same place, which is great—unless you need to end at a different point. If that is the case, quilt a filler design inside the star. This will allow you to work your way to a different corner and add a custom look to your quilting.

Quilting a filler design gives you more choices about where to travel out of the block.

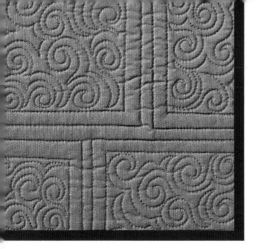

SYMMETRY ISN'T IMPORTANT WITH THIS BASIC DESIGN. THE MORE RANDOM THE PLACEMENT, THE BETTER THE RESULT. THIS DESIGN IS PERFECT FOR MEDIUM TO LARGE SQUARES, ESPECIALLY ONES THAT ARE TOO LARGE TO FIT WITHIN YOUR SEWING MACHINE.

VARIATIONS

If you aren't a fan of free-motion quilting and want to stick with just straight lines, you can omit the swirls and add more echo lines.

You can substitute more echoed lines for the swirly filler quilting.

You can also use this design to combine smaller blocks, giving it a symmetrical layout. Try alternating between fillers for a different look altogether.

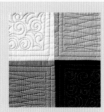

To tie the squares of a Four-Patch block together, quilt echoing lines along the inside corners of each square and fill in the outer corners with alternating designs.

SQUARE 8

Start

1. Starting from a random point on any side of the square, quilt a line that goes toward the center and then up to the side of the block. Travel along the edge of the block and echo ½˝ inside the previously quilted lines.

2. Fill inside the square with the quilting design of your choice. In this example, I used a swirl meander design ending at the top of the square.

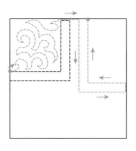

3. Travel along the edge until you are about ½˝ past the quilted lines, then repeat Steps 1 and 2 to quilt the next quarter of the block. To give this design a wonky or off-center look, don't line up the sections in the block center.

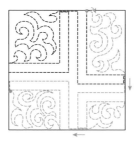

4. Continue filling in the block by outlining sections and filling them in.

note When you quilt the last two sections, make sure you line up their inside lines with the previously quilted sections. This will ensure that the block is filled in completely.

SQUARE 9

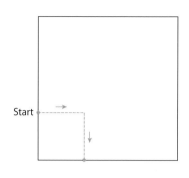

1. Quilt a small square in any corner. Adjusting the starting point depending on the size of the block, quilt a line over and down to complete the sides of a square.

THE BEAUTY OF THIS DESIGN ISN'T JUST IN THE ILLUSION OF DEPTH BUT ALSO IN THE CHARMING PATTERNS YOU CAN MAKE BY CHANGING UP THE PLACEMENT OF THE SMALLER BLOCK. THE DESIGN WORKS IN SQUARES OF ALMOST ALL SIZES, MAKING IT A VERSATILE DESIGN.

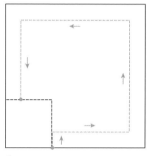

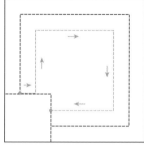

2. Travel back up the quilted line about ½″ and echo the sides of the block until you run into the square quilted in Step 1.

3. Travel along the edge of the quilted square (toward the center of the square) about ½″ and echo the inside of the lines quilted in Step 2.

note If you want to move on to the next block, just travel along the edge of the quilted square until you get to the edge of the block. Then you can either travel along the side of the block or move right into quilting the area around the block.

VARIATIONS

If you quilt this design in adjacent squares, you can alternate the placement of the smaller square to create a secondary design.

Once you get the hang of this design, you can fill in each of the sections with other quilting designs to really customize the look.

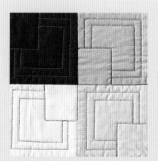

Alternate the placement of the small square in adjacent blocks to create a secondary pattern.

Fill in the smaller square with a free-motion quilting design.

Fill the larger square with a different design.

SQUARE 10

THIS DESIGN ACTUALLY PULLS DOUBLE DUTY. IT FITS PERFECTLY INTO RECTANGLES AND CAN BE MIRROR-IMAGED TO WORK IN SQUARES AS WELL. IT LOOKS A LOT MORE DIFFICULT THAN IT ACTUALLY IS AND CAN CREATE SOME INTERESTING SECONDARY DESIGNS.

1. Starting from any corner, quilt a diagonal line to the center of the opposite side and up to the opposite top corner.

2. Quilt a diagonal line down to about 1″ above the bottom of the V and back to the first corner.

3. Travel along the top edge of the block about 1″. Quilt another diagonal line to touch the bottom of the V you quilted in Step 2 and back up to about 1″ inside the opposite corner.

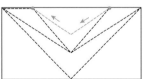

4. Quilt a diagonal line down to about 1″ above the bottom of the V and back to the starting point of Step 3.

TIP

If you want to fill in more of the block, try adding a diagonal line at the beginning and end of the design.

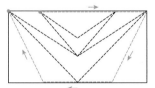

Start and end about equal distance from a corner and the block center for this variation.

VARIATIONS

I love to use this design to frame other blocks. It really helps draw the eye to that area.

You can also use this in differently shaped blocks as well.

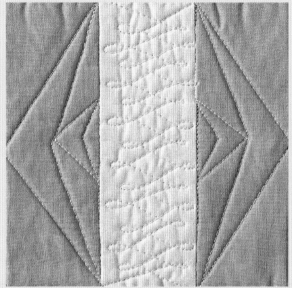

Try using this design to frame other blocks.

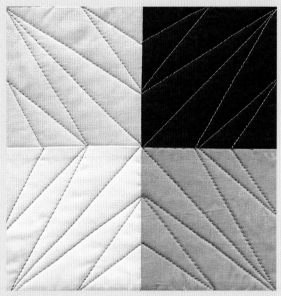

The Square 10 design in a square block

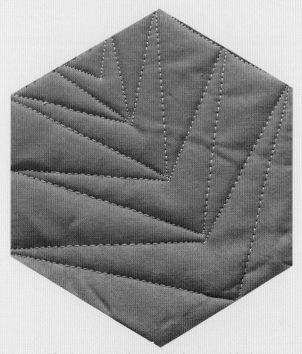

The Square 10 design in a hexagon block

TRIANGLES

Designed and pieced by Ruth Doss and quilted by Angela Walters

When I think of triangle blocks, some classic blocks come to mind instantly, including half-square triangles, Flying Geese, or setting triangles. But if you look closely enough, you can find triangle shapes in other areas as well. For instance, larger diamonds and squares can be divided into triangles.

But no matter where you find triangles on your quilts, this section has several designs to spark your creativity.

Does the Shape Matter?

There are different types of triangles. Most of the designs in this chapter will work for any kind of triangle. If you aren't sure if a design will fit a particular block, try drawing it with pencil and paper first.

WHEN IT COMES TO CHOOSING QUILTING DESIGNS, I TEND TO THINK, "THE MORE, THE MERRIER." IN THIS DESIGN, I'VE COMBINED A FEW BASIC QUILTING DESIGNS TO CREATE A PATTERN THAT REALLY BRINGS ATTENTION TO THE BLOCK. IT'S ESPECIALLY GREAT FOR LARGER BLOCKS, SUCH AS SETTING TRIANGLES, SINCE YOU CAN DIVIDE THE QUILTING INTO SMALLER SECTIONS.

VARIATIONS

To put your own twist on this design, try using different filler designs.

Here the lower triangle is filled with Triangle 5 (page 40).

Add more lines, then quilt this smaller triangle with a contrasting filler.

TRIANGLE 1

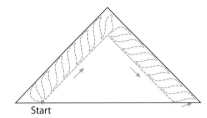

Start

1. Starting about 1″–2″ away from the bottom corner of the triangle, quilt a line that echoes the top sides of the triangle. Fill in the space between the edge of the block and the quilted line with a serpentine quilting line, returning to the starting point.

note Refer to Wavy Serpentine Lines (page 94) for tips on quilting a serpentine line.

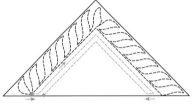

2. Travel along the bottom of the triangle about ¼″ and echo the first line from Step 1. Travel back ¼″ along the bottom of the triangle and echo the line again.

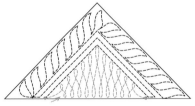

3. Fill in the resulting smaller triangle with the quilting design of your choice. I used a wishbone quilting design, one of my favorites. I love how it easily fills the triangle and contrasts with the serpentine pattern at the top of the triangle.

TRIANGLE 2

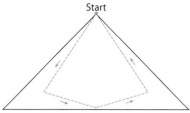

1. Starting from the top corner, quilt a line that angles down and stops about 1″ from the bottom left corner, then continues down to the halfway point of the bottom edge. Repeat on the opposite side of the triangle to return to the starting point.

WHILE THIS DESIGN MIGHT LOOK BASIC BY ITSELF, IT REALLY SHINES WHEN USED IN CONSECUTIVE BLOCKS. THIS IS ONE OF MY FAVORITE DESIGNS TO USE IN THE SIDE TRIANGLES OF THE FLYING GEESE BLOCKS.

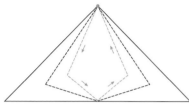

2. Echo inside the previously quilted line, coming to a point at the top and bottom of the block.

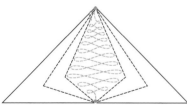

3. Fill in the space in the inner shape. In this example I used a wishbone design (one of my favorites!). Of course, you could use any other quilting design or even quilt a straight line.

VARIATIONS

To fill in larger triangles or to switch things up a bit, add more echo lines inside the design and try a different filler design.

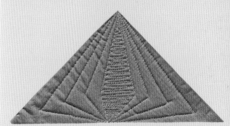

Try stitching a back-and-forth line as a filler.

A straight line also helps fill the space.

MOST OF MY DESIGNS ARE FAIRLY BASIC, CONSISTING OF JUST A FEW STEPS. BUT THAT DOESN'T LIMIT THEIR IMPACT ON A QUILT. THIS DESIGN IS THE PERFECT EXAMPLE—JUST A COUPLE OF ECHO LINES AND A FILLER—BUT ITS BEAUTY SHOWS WHEN IT IS USED TO CREATE SECONDARY PATTERNS. LET ME SHOW YOU WHAT I MEAN!

VARIATIONS

You can easily make this design fit your preferences by adding more echo lines, spacing them out farther, or exchanging the wishbone for something else.

Add more echo lines.

Alternate the placement of the echo line in the corner of a quilt.

TRIANGLE 3

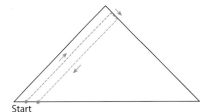

Start

1. Starting about ¼″ from a bottom corner of the triangle, echo a short side of the triangle. Travel ¼″ along the edge of the block and echo the previously quilted line.

TIP

Depending on the size of the block, you could echo it several times.

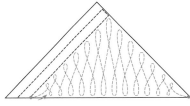

2. Fill in the smaller triangle with the quilting design of your choice. I really like using the wishbone design for this step. It moves me on to the opposite point of the block (allowing me to continue on to the next one) and also contrasts nicely with the echo lines.

Like I said, it's nice and basic! But when you use this design in adjacent blocks, such as setting triangles, alternating the placement makes a unusual secondary effect.

Use the design to frame a square quilt block.

Radiate the echo lines.

TRIANGLE 4

1. Start halfway between the points of a short side and quilt a diagonal line ending halfway between the points of the long side. Quilt another diagonal line ending halfway between the points of the other short side of the triangle.

2. Now that you have 3 little sections—2 triangles and a square—it's time to fill them in! In the square, quilt a diamond shape that touches the first starting point in Step 1 and returns to the starting point on the right side of the block.

3. Travel along the side of the triangle until you are at the nearest bottom point. Quilt a continuous curved line that goes from point to point, ending at the bottom of the square you just quilted. Quilt the remaining triangle the same way, ending on the opposite point from which you started.

I LIKE TO USE QUILTING TO DIVIDE BLOCKS INTO OTHER SHAPES. THIS DESIGN IS A GREAT EXAMPLE OF THAT. IT'S BASIC, BUT QUICK, AND GREAT FOR TRIANGLES OF MOST SIZES.

VARIATIONS

This design looks especially interesting when it's used in a continuous layout.

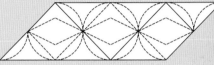

Alternate the design in rows.

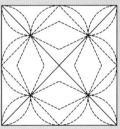

Rotate the placement in quarter squares.

And of course, try using different quilting designs within the shapes.

I rearranged the shapes from Triangle 4 to make a new variation.

THIS IS A FUNKY, GEOMETRIC DESIGN.

TRIANGLE 5

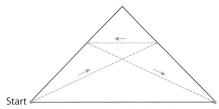

1. Quilt a diagonal line from a bottom point of the triangle to 1″–2″ from the top point. Quilt a line parallel to the bottom of the triangle, ending on the other side of the triangle. Stitch another diagonal line to the opposite bottom point.

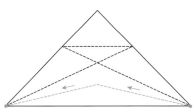

2. For bigger blocks, or if you need to return to your starting point, you can quilt 2 diagonal lines underneath the design.

This design can be used in other block shapes as well. Try it in squares or even hexagons.

VARIATION

For larger triangles, repeat Step 1 a couple times, really filling in the area.

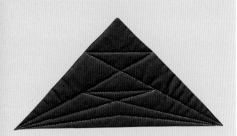

Fill in by repeating Step 1.

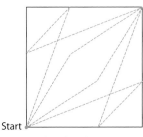

Echo the design in a square block.

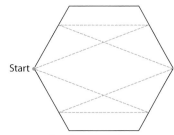

The design makes a nice filler in hexagon blocks.

TRIANGLE 6

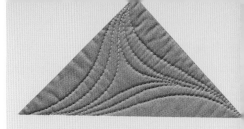

1. Quilt a line that gently curves up and back down from one corner to the next.

Start

SOMETIMES YOU JUST NEED A QUICK DESIGN TO FILL IN LITTLE TRIANGLES. THIS IS THE PERFECT DESIGN TO DO JUST THAT. THIS DESIGN, A VARIATION OF THE CONTINUOUS CURVE TECHNIQUE, HAS BEEN AROUND FOR A LONG TIME AND IS BY NO MEANS ORIGINAL TO ME. IT ADDS SUCH A FUN, CURVED LOOK TO TRIANGLES OF ANY SIZE THAT I JUST HAD TO INCLUDE IT IN THIS BOOK!

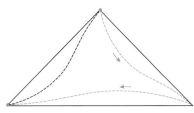

2. Quilt your way around the block, working from corner to corner, until you get to the starting point.

TIP

Making the highest part of the curve closer to the beginning will leave room for the next curve.

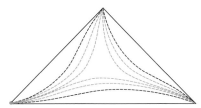

3. For larger blocks or a denser design, you can echo the lines, coming to the corner each time.

VARIATIONS

This works in any block with corners. Try it in a variety of shapes.

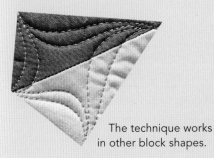

The technique works in other block shapes.

Or, instead of working your way around the whole block, just quilt 2 sides of a block for a slightly different variation.

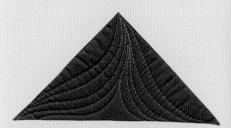

Try quilting just 2 sides of a block.

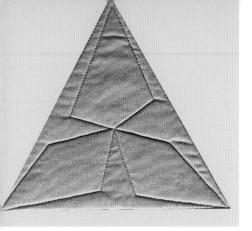

THIS ANGULAR-LOOKING DESIGN LOOKS GREAT IN LARGE EQUILATERAL TRIANGLES. DEFINITELY DON'T TRY TO SQUEEZE THIS DESIGN INTO TINY TRIANGLES. IT STARTS AND ENDS AT THE SAME SPOT, MAKING IT EASY TO MOVE ON TO THE NEXT BLOCK— ESPECIALLY HELPFUL WHEN QUILTING TRIANGLES THAT ARE IN A ROW.

VARIATION

If you like a lot of quilting like me, adding more echo lines is a great way to add more detail to the design. I quilted the entire design first and then echoed it.

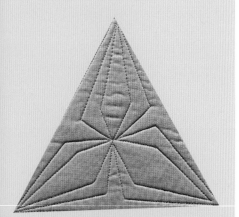

Echo the lines to add detail.

TRIANGLE 7

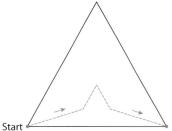

Start

1. From any corner, quilt a line that angles out to a point and up to the middle of the block. Quilt the reverse shape on to the next corner.

note Don't stress out too much about getting the notch perfectly in the center. I try to focus on making the notches in the next steps touch instead.

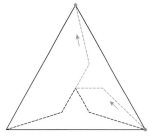 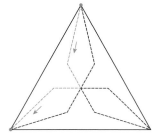

2. Repeat Step 1 on the remaining sides of the triangle, trying to keep it as symmetrical as possible.

TIP

While this design looks fairly basic, I struggled with getting the proportions right. If you find it difficult to keep the shapes symmetrical, try marking the design the first few times.

TRIANGLE 8

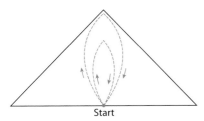

1. Starting at the halfway point of the long side, quilt an oval shape that almost touches the opposite point. Echo inside the oval to add a little more detail.

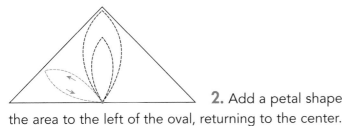

2. Add a petal shape to fill in the area to the left of the oval, returning to the center.

VARIATION

Echo around the outside of the shape to fill in larger triangles or any unquilted areas.

Fill in by echoing the outside of the ovals.

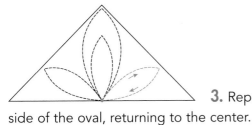

3. Repeat Step 2 on the other side of the oval, returning to the center.

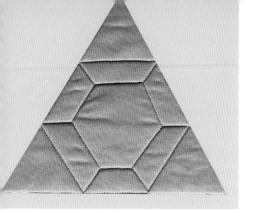

I LOVE USING QUILTING TO CHANGE THE LOOK OF A BLOCK. THIS BASIC DESIGN TURNS A TRIANGLE INTO A HEXAGON. IT CAN CHANGE THE WHOLE LOOK OF THE QUILT WITH JUST A COUPLE OF LINES. TO GET A SYMMETRICAL DESIGN, USE IT IN EQUILATERAL TRIANGLES.

VARIATIONS

You can use any design to fill in the hexagon. In this variation, I used Hexagon 2 (page 73). If your block is large enough, you can fill in the triangles as well.

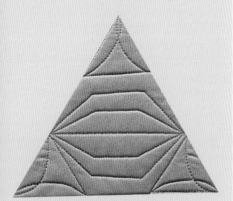

Use any hexagon design as a filler.

TRIANGLE 9

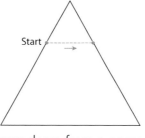

1. Starting about a third of the way down from a corner, quilt a straight line across to the same point on the other side.

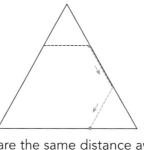

2. Travel along the edge until you are the same distance away from the next corner. Repeat Step 1.

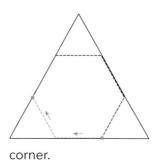

3. Repeat Step 2 with the last corner.

4. Fill in the hexagon shape with the design of your choice.

TRIANGLE 10

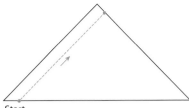

Start

1. Starting about 1˝ away from a bottom corner, quilt a line that echoes a short side of the block. Travel about 1˝ back along the line.

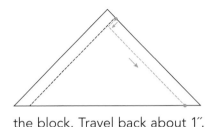

2. Echo the next side of the block. Travel back about 1˝.

3. Repeat Steps 1 and 2, working your way into the center of the triangle.

note Even though I worked my way around the block clockwise, you could quilt in the other direction as well.

COMBINING STRAIGHT LINES WITH JUST A LITTLE BIT OF TRAVELING RESULTS IN A DESIGN THAT ADDS A LOOK OF DEPTH TO YOUR QUILTING. IF YOU AREN'T A FAN OF TRAVELING ALONG PREVIOUSLY QUILTED LINES, DON'T WORRY—IT'S JUST A LITTLE BIT. THE RESULT IS WELL WORTH THE EXTRA STEP. THIS WORKS IN TRIANGLES OF ALL SHAPES AND SIZES.

VARIATIONS

Try quilting the lines closer or farther apart, depending on the size of the block. In this example, the lines are about ¼˝ apart.

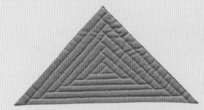

Change the space between lines to fit the size of the block.

You can also get a nice effect by varying the spacing within the block. As I worked my way toward the inside of the block, I quilted the lines closer and closer.

For a different look, vary the spacing between lines.

CIRCLES

Designed by Natalie Barnes, pieced by Ruth Doss, and quilted by Angela Walters

Piecing curved blocks, such as circles, can seem such a daunting task to many quilters. But machine quilting them doesn't have to be a difficulty. In fact, this whole section is dedicated to designs that are perfect for circles.

Types of Circle Blocks

Circle-shaped blocks come in several types, whether appliqué or pieced. The designs in this chapter are geared toward slightly large blocks. When I work on a quilt of small appliquéd circles, for instance 1″–2″ circles, I keep the quilting fairly basic. But I tend to like more quilting in larger blocks, which is why I chose these particular designs.

Of course, I have included variations for most of the designs. I hope you will find a few that will be perfect for your next circle quilt.

Tips for Quilting Curves

A lot of the designs in this section contain curves, mostly due the curvy shape of a circle. If your curves are looking a little squared off, here are a few tips to make the quilting go a little smoother.

▶ DON'T AUTO-CORRECT.

Instead of trying to "correct" your curve while quilting, focus on getting a smooth movement. Even if it isn't perfect, the smoothness of the line will give the illusion that it's just right.

▶ SPEED UP…A BIT.

Sometimes quilters think that they can get a nice, quilted curve if they just slow down. But that's not the case. Instead, try to speed up the machine a bit so that the momentum of the quilting carries you through the curve. But don't go so fast that you feel out of control.

▶ LOOK AHEAD.

Instead of looking directly at the needle, look ahead a couple of inches. Trust that your hands will carry you to your point. It may sound counterintuitive, but there's a good chance that it will help you.

▶ TURN OFF THE REGULATOR.

If you use a stitch regulator and are having a trouble with the curves, try switching into manual mode. For some quilters, the movement of the machine will feel a little different and it will be easier to get nice, curvy designs. Does that mean that your stitches won't all be the same length? It sure does, but I don't worry about that!

Ready? Let's get started!

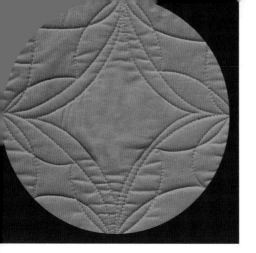

CIRCLE 1

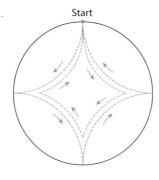

Start

1. From the top, quilt a curved line that goes to the middle of the side, to the bottom, and to the next side, returning to the top. Echo inside of the design, returning to the starting point.

THIS CURVY DESIGN ADDS A LOT OF DETAIL TO YOUR CIRCLES, A PLUS FOR LARGER BLOCKS. WHILE MARKING ISN'T NECESSARY, YOU COULD MAKE SMALL MARKS AT THE TOP, BOTTOM, AND THE CENTER SIDES OF THE BLOCKS TO HELP KEEP IT SYMMETRICAL.

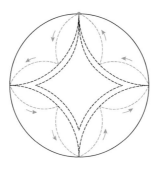

2. Quilt a curved line to the middle of the previously quilted curve, then on to the next point. Continue working around the quilt, quilting curved lines until you return to the starting point.

VARIATIONS

Experiment with the fillers and echo lines to come up with your own variations.

Different fillers and echoes make interesting variations.

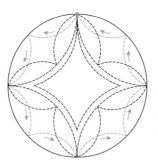

3. Work around the block again, repeating Step 2 but with the middle point touching the outside of the circle.

This design works in square blocks as well.

Try the design in a square.

4. You could also leave out the curved lines and use a different design around the curve. The possibilities are endless!

CIRCLE 2

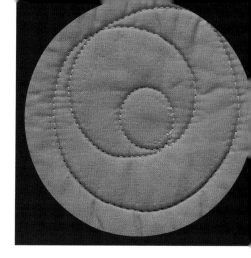

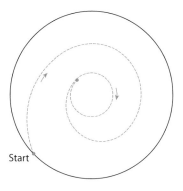

1. Starting from any point on the edge of the circle, quilt a line that curls in toward the center and ends in a circle.

THIS DESIGN ADDS A GROOVY LOOK TO YOUR CIRCLE BLOCKS AND IS GREAT FOR SMALL OR MEDIUM CIRCLES. IT HAS A DIFFERENT LOOK THAN JUST QUILTING A SWIRL IN THE CENTER OF THE CIRCLE, BUT IS JUST AS EASY TO DO.

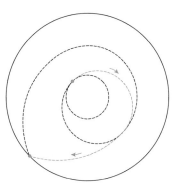

2. Work your way out of the swirl by quilting a line that curls away from the center circle, crossing the line across from it until you reach the outside of the circle.

VARIATION

Add a filler design in between the outer line and the edge of the block.

For bigger circles, add more circles.

Fill in the outer block with a curvy design.

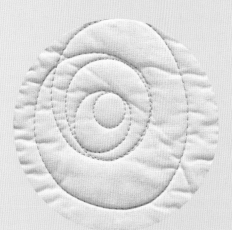

If you have more space, add more circles in the center.

THIS FERNLIKE DESIGN DIVIDES THE BLOCK IN HALF AND ADDS A CUSTOM LOOK TO YOUR QUILTING. IT IS PERFECT FOR LARGER BLOCKS OR IN AREAS THAT YOU WANT TO HIGHLIGHT.

CIRCLE 3

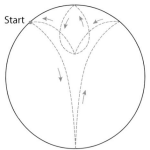

1. Quilt a line that curves from the edge of the circle to the bottom and back up to the opposite side. Quilt a flowerlike shape in the top of the circle by quilting a line that curves down to the center, up to the top and back, and on to the other side.

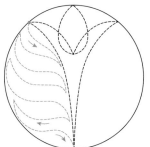

2. Quilt fernlike leaves down 1 side of the circle. Extend the leaves to almost touch the edge of the block. Continue until you reach the bottom.

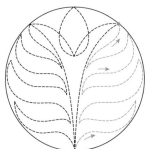

3. Quilt your way back up the other side of the block, mirroring the leaf shapes from Step 2.

VARIATIONS

If those fern-like shapes give you trouble, just add another curved line to fill in the block.

Stitch another curved line instead of the fern leaves.

Or if you love quilting feathers, replace the ferns with feathers for a softer look.

Quilt feathers instead of ferns.

CIRCLE 4

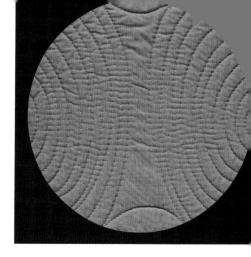

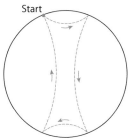

1. Starting at one edge of the circle, quilt a narrow, curved rectangle with points touching the edge of the circle. When you complete the circle, you will have returned to the starting point.

I LIKE HOW THIS DESIGN "DECONSTRUCTS" THE CIRCLE SHAPE BY CHANGING UP THE CURVES. IMAGINE JUST HOW GOOD IT WOULD LOOK WHEN QUILTED IN ADJACENT CIRCLES. IT CAN BE TEMPTING TO FRET OVER THE PERFECTION OF THE CURVES IN THIS DESIGN, BUT WHEN IT'S FINISHED ALL YOU WILL SEE IS THE TEXTURE OF THE QUILTING.

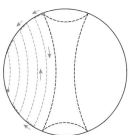

2. On 1 side of the block, stitch a series of curved lines to echo a long side of the rectangle. Travel along the edge of the circle between echo lines.

VARIATIONS

Quilt the design twice in a circle, alternating the direction.

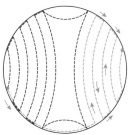

3. Travel along the edge of the circle to get to the opposite side. Repeat Step 2 to fill in the block.

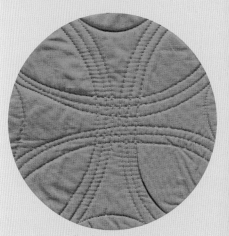

Add even more quilting inside the rectangle.

4. If you wish to add more quilting, fill in the curved rectangle with a design of your choice.

For really dense quilting, add another echoed curved rectangle in an alternating direction.

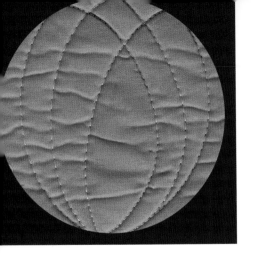

JUST A FEW CURVED LINES MAKE UP THIS DESIGN, BUT ALTERNATING THE DIRECTION REALLY HELPS THE DESIGN WORK ON CIRCLES OF ALL SIZES. EXPERIMENT WITH THE SPACING AND NUMBER OF LINES TO MAKE THIS DESIGN YOUR OWN.

VARIATIONS

Fill in the space between the curves for a different look.

Add a filler in the center.

This design looks great in hexagon blocks as well.

Try this design in a hexagon.

CIRCLE 5

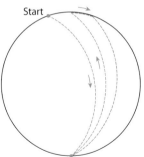

1. Starting toward the top of the circle, quilt a gentle curve to the bottom. Quilt another line that curves out and ends ½˝ away from the starting point. Travel along the edge of the circle and quilt another line that curves back to the bottom.

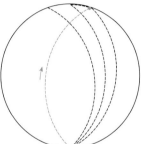

2. Quilt a line that curves from the bottom out in the opposite direction.

note Sometimes I make the point touch at the top and sometimes I don't. It's fine either way!

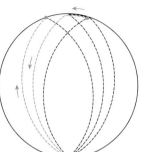

3. Travel along the edge and quilt a line that curves to the bottom and back up about ½˝ away.

CIRCLE 6

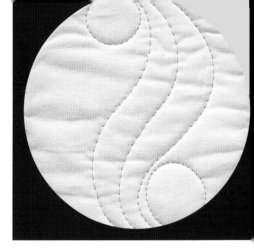

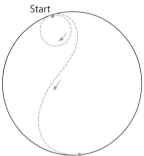

1. Quilt a small circle near the top of the circle block. It should just touch the edge of the circle. Continue stitching to the opposite side of the block in an S curve.

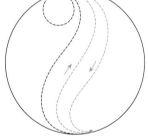

2. Echo the curve back up to the top, tucking it around the quilted circle. Echo again back to the bottom of the circle block.

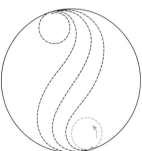

3. Quilt a small circle at the bottom edge of the block.

THIS DESIGN, INSPIRED BY YIN AND YANG, WILL LEAVE YOUR QUILT BLOCK LOOKING NICE AND BALANCED. I LIKE TO USE THIS DESIGN IN SMALLER BLOCKS BUT WILL SHOW YOU SOME VARIATIONS FOR LARGER BLOCKS.

VARIATIONS

I love adding echoing to embellish any design, but it definitely looks great on this one. It's especially great for larger circle blocks.

Echo quilting really enhances this design.

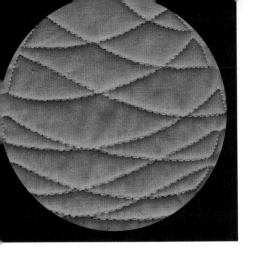

IT'S NO SECRET THAT I LOVE THE WISHBONE DESIGN. I USE IT ALL THE TIME. WHAT CAN I SAY? IT FITS IN SO MANY SHAPES AND AREAS. THIS DESIGN IS A WISHBONE DESIGN WITH A SLIGHT VARIATION, HELPING IT FIT A CIRCLE BLOCK.

VARIATIONS

Try curving the lines so that they are opposite of the block curve.

Arc the outer lines away from the edge of the block.

CIRCLE 7

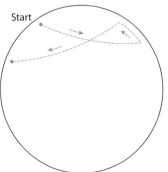

1. Starting from any side, quilt a line that angles down, stopping just short of the edge. Echo the curve of the circle up about a ¼″ and then angle down in the opposite direction.

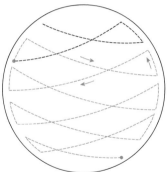

2. Continue working your way down the block, curving the edges of the outer design so that they echo the sides of the block. Make the curves as close or as far apart as you prefer.

CIRCLE 8

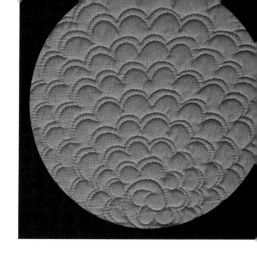

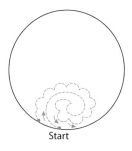

1. Quilt a small curl close the edge of the circle block. Work your way back around the outside of the curl by quilting small arcs to resemble petals.

Start

I HAVE USED THIS FLOWER DESIGN AS A MEANDER DESIGN MORE TIMES THAN I CAN COUNT. NOW IT'S TIME TO USE IT TO HIGHLIGHT A CIRCLE BLOCK. THIS IS A FORGIVING DESIGN, SO JUMP RIGHT IN AND GET STARTED.

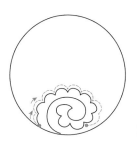

2. Echo back around the petals.

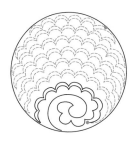

3. Once you get to the edge of the block, quilt another row of arc-shaped petals and echo your way back to the other side. Continue quilting rows until you reach the top of the block.

note Try to keep the arcs as consistent as possible. This will ensure that the texture of this design really shows up in your block.

VARIATIONS

Instead of quilting the rows all the way to the top of the block, you can stop halfway through and add a different design, such as leaves.

If you don't mind starting and stopping, you can start the flower in the center of the block. It will really add a focal point to your blocks.

Or, forget the flower altogether and turn those arcs into clamshells to give your larger circle blocks a textured look.

Add a different design in half of the block.

Put the flower in the center of the circle.

Stitch clamshells in larger circles.

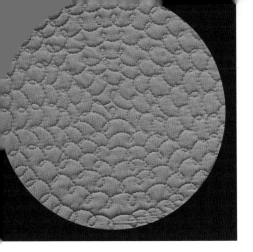

CIRCLE 9

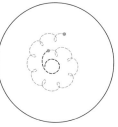

I LOVE THE LOOK OF SPIRALS ON CIRCLE BLOCKS, BUT SOMETIMES, KEEPING THOSE CURVED LINES NICE AND SMOOTH CAN BE A PAIN. THIS DESIGN TAKES THE BASIC IDEA OF A SPIRAL AND CHANGES IT UP A BIT BY INCORPORATING LOOPS. IT'S GREAT FOR LARGER CIRCLES AND ESPECIALLY EASY TO QUILT. GIVE IT A TRY!

1. Starting from the block center (or somewhat close), quilt a small circle that extends past itself.

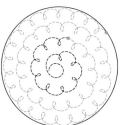

2. Begin quilting loops that wrap around the circle.

VARIATION

It is easy to customize this design by adding different elements! For instance, to really pull your eye to the block, quilt a large, offset spiral and surround it with loops.

An off-center spiral contrasts with the surrounding loops.

3. Continue quilting loops around and around until you fill in the entire quilt block.

TIP

I like to alternate the direction of the loops, but you could keep them all going the same way if you would like.

Alternating the direction of the loops allows the rows to stick closer together.

CIRCLE 10

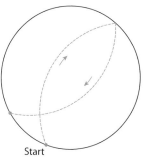

Start

1. Quilt a curved line that reaches the other side of the circle and curves back about 1″ away from the starting point.

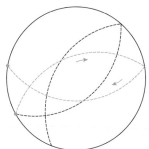

2. Quilt another curved line that touches the other side about 1″ away from the previously quilted line. Curve back so that you are touching about 1″ from where you started.

VARIATIONS

You can change the look of the design by quilting the curves so that they are closer together or farther apart.

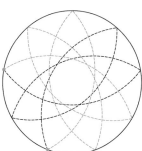

3. Continue working your way around the block, quilting petals about 1″ apart.

Change the spacing of the curves to vary the design.

DIAMONDS

Night Sky, designed by Julie Herman, pieced by Ruth Doss, and quilted by Angela Walters

About This Chapter

Diamond blocks are fairly common in the quilting universe. Just walk around any quilt show and you might see Lone Star quilts or other star blocks made from diamond shapes. Having a few go-to designs for diamonds will make your quilting go a little smoother.

About the Designs

The best quilting designs are versatile, easily used on several different shapes. In this section, perhaps more than others, I show how the designs can be used in a lot of different ways. Even if you don't have any star-shaped blocks in your quilting future, designs in this section are just begging to be used on your quilts.

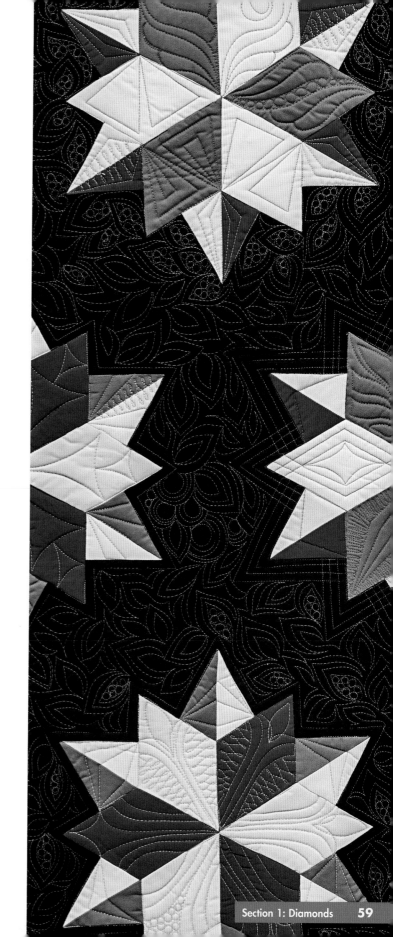

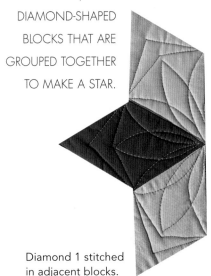

DIAMOND 1

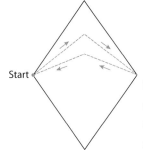

Start

1. Starting from a side corner, quilt a line that angles up to about ½˝ from the top corner and then on to the next side corner. Echo back, returning to the starting corner.

THIS DESIGN COMBINES GEOMETRIC AND CURVY LINES TO MAKE A DESIGN THAT IS PERFECT FOR DIAMOND BLOCKS. IT MOVES FROM ONE SIDE TO THE NEXT, MAKING IT GREAT FOR DIAMOND-SHAPED BLOCKS THAT ARE GROUPED TOGETHER TO MAKE A STAR.

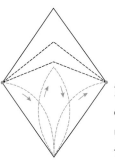

2. Quilt a continuous curve design by quilting a curve to the bottom corner, up toward the top and back, and on to the next corner.

Diamond 1 stitched in adjacent blocks.

VARIATIONS

Replace the continuous curve design with straight lines for a more geometric design.

Try it out in differently shaped blocks.

Try switching the sides to give it a different look.

Use straight lines instead of curves.

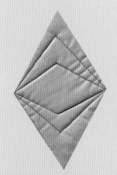

Diamond 1 in a half-square triangle block

Create a new look by rotating the design.

DIAMOND 2

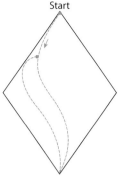

Start

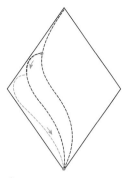

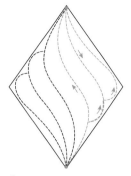

1. Quilt a gentle S shape from the top or bottom corner to the opposite corner. Quilt a petal-like shape that touches the first line.

2. Travel back along the petal, until you have room to quilt another petal shape. Quilt the new petal, returning to the same starting corner.

3. Echo the S curve on the other side of the diamond corner and repeat Steps 1 and 2 to fill the block.

THE FAUX ROPE DESIGN MIGHT LOOK FAMILIAR SINCE IT WAS IN MY FIRST BOOK, *SHAPE BY SHAPE FREE-MOTION QUILTING WITH ANGELA WALTERS*, BUT IT WORKS SO WELL IN DIAMOND BLOCKS THAT I JUST HAD TO INCLUDE IT IN THIS SECTION. IT ADDS A CURVY, ELEGANT LOOK TO YOUR QUILT AND IS A FAVORITE OF MINE FOR BLOCKS THAT ARE 3″–6″ OR SO. THE DESIGN STARTS AND STOPS IN THE SAME PLACE, MAKING IT EASY TO STITCH BLOCKS THAT ARE IN ROWS.

VARIATIONS

If you are working with large diamonds or you want to add an extra detail, you can fill in between the lines of the stem with pebbles. It might take a little longer, but it really looks nice!

If you want a curvier look for your quilt, quilt a swirl that fills the top of the block and add petals to just one side of the design. This is a great way to practice the petal shapes without having to quilt so many of them!

TIP

Don't worry about making the petals the same shape. Instead, just try to fill in the block as much as possible.

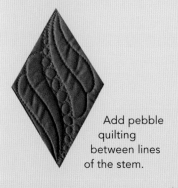

Add pebble quilting between lines of the stem.

DIAMOND 3

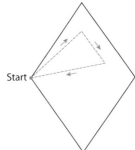

1. Starting from a side corner, quilt a triangle that fills the top half of the diamond, returning to the starting point.

I LOVE IT WHEN A QUILTING DESIGN CAN CHANGE UP THE LOOK OF A QUILT BLOCK, EVEN IF IT IS JUST A LITTLE BIT! THIS DESIGN IS FAIRLY BASIC, BUT ALTERNATING THE DIRECTION OF THE INDIVIDUAL PARTS OF THE DESIGN MAKES IT LOOK MORE COMPLEX. I USE THIS DESIGN IN BLOCKS OF ALL SIZES.

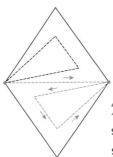

2. Quilt a horizontal line to the opposite side corner and quilt another triangle shape to fill in the bottom half of the block.

note I like to stitch in the seams of all my quilts, so I would do that before I quilt this design. But that is definitely a step that you could leave out!

VARIATIONS

For larger blocks, you can echo inside the triangles before moving on to the next step.

If you have room, echo inside the triangles.

For a different look altogether, you can leave out the horizontal line and just quilt 2 triangles that are facing the same direction.

Make both triangles radiate from the same corner.

Try using this design in triangles to give your blocks a different look.

This shape works well in a half-square triangle.

DIAMOND 4

1. Quilt the stem by stitching a wavy line from the bottom corner to near the top corner. Quilt the first petal by echoing along the side of the block and returning to the stem.

Start

TIP
When returning to the stem, try quilting the line so that it looks as though it will merge into the stem.

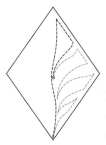

2. Continue working your way down the side of the stem by quilting petals that fill in the space.

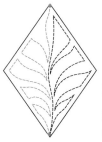

3. Echo up the other side of the stem. Quilt petals along the left side, returning to the starting point.

note I echo the side of the stem because I have an easier time quilting petals starting at the top and working my way to the bottom. If you want, you can leave the echo out.

SOMETIMES I WANT TO QUILT SOMETHING THAT IS QUICK AND CURVY, AND THIS DESIGN IS JUST PERFECT! IT'S A LITTLE FERNY, A LITTLE FEATHERY, AND A LOT OF FUN!

VARIATIONS

If you just love the way this design looks, you can use it as a border design.

Start

Use the same technique to stitch a border design.

And since I love echoing, sometimes I will echo inside each of the petals before moving on.

Everything is better with echoes! If you have room, echo inside each petal.

I ALWAYS SAY THAT ECHOING IS YOUR FRIEND! ECHOING THE SIDES OF A QUILT BLOCK IS AN EASY WAY TO MAKE THE SHAPE OF THE BLOCK STAND OUT, AND THIS DESIGN IS A PERFECT EXAMPLE. SIMPLY ECHOING OPPOSITE EDGES OF THE BLOCK RESULTS IN A LATTICE-LIKE PATTERN THAT IS PERFECT FOR ALL KINDS OF QUILTS.

DIAMOND 5

1. Start about ¼″ from the top corner and echo along the left side of the block. Travel along the edge and echo 2 more times.

note I tend to quilt lines in groups of three, but of course you could do more or less, depending on what works for you.

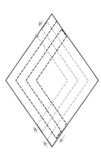

2. Travel back along the side of the block so that you are about ¼″ on the other side of the starting corner. Repeat Step 1 by echoing the opposite side of the block.

VARIATIONS

You can add a little extra flourish by quilting a design in the center before finishing the last line.

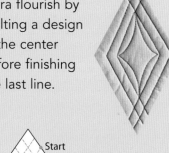

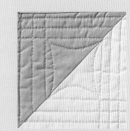

When quilting the last echo line, stop when it touches the first echo line. Fill in square, return to the point, and finish the last line.

Even though I have this design in the diamond section, I really like to use it in outside blocks as well.

Diamond pattern around the points of a star

Of course, this works for any block with sides.

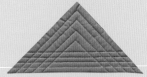

Diamond 5 in a half-square triangle

Diamond 5 in a triangle

DIAMOND 6

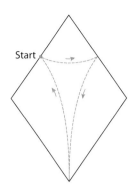

1. From halfway between the top corner and a side corner, quilt a line that curves across, stopping a couple inches away from the opposite side. Continue quilting a curvy line to the opposite side of the block and back to the starting point.

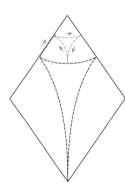

2. Travel along the side of the block, stopping about 1″ away from the top corner. Quilt a line that curves to the opposite side, down to the previous quilting, and back to the starting point. Continue quilting along the edge of the block to move on to the next block.

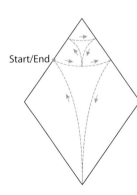

note I don't mind traveling in the seams, but that's just my personal preference. If you want, you can leave that part out. Just stop in the middle of the top curve in Step 1, quilt the smaller shape, and then complete the design.

It's hard to get an idea of just how beautiful this design is when you can see only a single diamond! Here is what it would like when used in diamond blocks that are arranged in a star formation.

I LOVE, LOVE, LOVE HOW THIS DESIGN LOOKS WHEN IT IS USED IN STAR BLOCKS. IT REALLY ADDS A SECONDARY DESIGN TO THE QUILT! TRY IT IN DIAMONDS OF ALL SIZES.

VARIATION

This design can make a curvy starlike shape as well. Just travel to the opposite corner from where you started and repeat Step 1.

The design really shines in a pieced star.

Stitch a star by repeating Step 1 from the opposite side.

DIAMOND 7

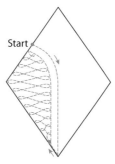

Start

1. Starting halfway between the top corner and a side corner, quilt a line that curves out and then down the center of the block, stopping at the bottom corner. Travel ¼″ along the edge and echo the side of the line. Work your way back toward the bottom corner, filling in between the echoed line and the edge of the block with a wishbone design.

I FIRST WORKED WITH THIS DESIGN ON A QUILT WITH GOTHIC ARCHES. I LOVE HOW THE PLAY ON A BASIC WISHBONE DESIGN JAZZES UP THE WHOLE BLOCK. SINCE THIS DESIGN HAS SEVERAL ELEMENTS, I PREFER TO USE IT IN LARGER DIAMOND SHAPES. BUT DON'T LET ALL THE STEPS KEEP YOU FROM TRYING THE DESIGN; IT'S JUST CURVED LINES AND WISHBONES!

note Of course, if you don't like the wishbone design, you can substitute with any filler design. The most important thing is that you end up at the bottom!

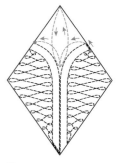

2. Quilt a line that travels up the center line and curves to the opposite side of the block. Echo the side of the line and quilt the wishbone design so that you end up near the top of the block.

3. Fill in the top of the block by quilting a continuous curve design.

VARIATIONS

If you don't like too much quilting or just want to leave out the wishbone design, you can replace it with an echo.

Replace the wishbone filler with echoed center lines.

You could also use this design in rectangle-shaped blocks.

It is easy to tweak the design to fit in rectangles.

If you need even more options, you can take out the continuous curve design in the top of the block and use a different design to fill it in.

Stitch your favorite filler instead of the continuous curve at the top.

DIAMOND 8

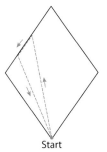

Start

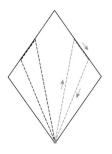

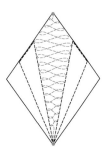

1. Starting from the bottom corner of the block, quilt a straight line that angles out to about 1″ away from an adjacent corner. Travel along the edge of the block about 1″ and stitch a straight line back to the starting point.

2. Repeat Step 1 on the other side of the block.

3. Quilt your way to the top corner using the design of your choice.

THIS DESIGN CAN SOFTEN THE ANGULAR SIDES OF A DIAMOND BLOCK BY ADDING A "RAY" EFFECT TO THE QUILT. IT'S ANOTHER EXAMPLE OF HOW BASIC SHAPES CAN MAKE AN IMPACT ON YOUR QUILTS.

VARIATIONS

A really easy way to quilt an interesting variation of this design is to switch up the lines and the fillers.

Try it in adjacent diamond blocks.

I also love how this design looks in other block shapes.

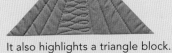

It also highlights a triangle block.

It's also great for irregularly shaped or uncommon blocks.

Diamond 8 adapts well to a kite-shaped block.

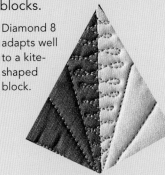

Switch the placement of the lines and the fillers for a different look.

Alternate the placement of straight lines and fillers in adjacent blocks.

Diamond 8 looks fantastic in a group of hexagons.

THIS DESIGN REALLY ENHANCES THE DIAMOND SHAPE BY USING THE EDGES OF THE BLOCK AS A GUIDE. IT WORKS BEST IN MEDIUM TO LARGER BLOCKS.

VARIATIONS

Try out all of your favorite fillers with this block. I personally like the wishbone design in some of my blocks.

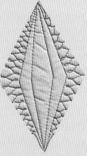

Choose any filler that will contrast with the echo lines.

Combine the regular design and the variation to give groups of blocks a different look.

In adjacent diamonds, alternate between the basic design and a variation.

DIAMOND 9

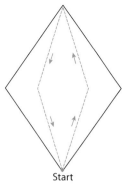

Start

1. Starting at the bottom corner, quilt a diamond that echoes the inside of the block and touches the top corner. Leave at least 1″ between the quilting line and the edge of the block.

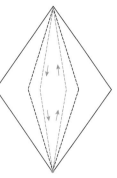

2. Echo inside the diamond, coming back to the starting point.

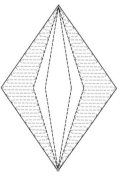

3. If you wish, quilt a filler between the outer line of quilting and the edges of the block. In this example, I used back-and-forth lines.

DIAMOND 10

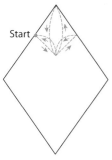

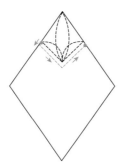

1. Starting 1″–2″ from a top corner, quilt a line that angles down toward the middle and back up to the opposite side. Fill in the space above with a continuous curve flower.

2. Travel along the edge and echo underneath the first line you quilted.

THIS DESIGN MIGHT APPEAR COMPLEX BECAUSE OF THE NUMBER OF STEPS REQUIRED, BUT IT ISN'T HARD AT ALL. IT'S BEST FOR LARGER BLOCKS.

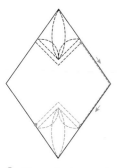

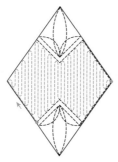

3. Travel along the edge of the block and repeat Steps 1 and 2 on the opposite corner of the block.

4. Travel to a side corner and fill in the area from side to side with a design.

VARIATIONS

Once you get the basic idea of the steps, you can create some fun variations.

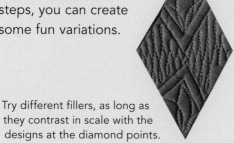

Try different fillers, as long as they contrast in scale with the designs at the diamond points.

Look at the elegant secondary pattern when you use it in a star formation!

The easy-to-stitch block elements create a wonderful secondary pattern in a star.

HEXAGONS

Pieced by Ruth Doss and quilted by Angela Walters

Since hexagons can range in size, I have tried to include designs that work for most. But the focus is mostly on designs that work best on midsize to large blocks. When quilting small hexagon blocks, such as Grandmother's Flower Garden, I like to use designs that are more basic.

Think in Multiples

Hexagons are somewhat unusual in that they are almost always part of a bigger pattern. Rarely will I come across a quilt with a hexagon by itself. When you choose a quilting design for your hexagons, consider what they will look like in the context of your quilt pattern. There is a good chance that when the design is repeated, it will create a secondary design. That's an exciting element of quilting, seeing unexpected patterns emerge!

I have included some examples of the designs stitched in different groups, but your imagination might be even better than mine!

Don't Choose Just One

Since I can get bored easily when quilting the same design over and over, I like to use more than one design. Hexagon blocks are great for doing just that. Find a couple of designs that look interesting and try both of them within the pieced motif.

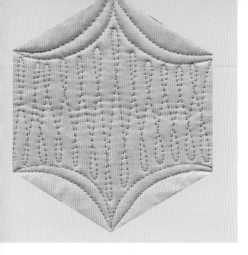

THIS DESIGN COMBINES TWO OF MY FAVORITE DESIGNS—THE CONTINUOUS CURVE AND THE WISHBONE. EVEN THOUGH I LIKE HOW IT LOOKS ON ITS OWN, I THINK IT LOOKS ESPECIALLY WONDERFUL WHEN USED IN HEXAGONS IN ROWS. YOU CAN QUICKLY QUILT A WHOLE SECTION AT ONCE. NOW THAT'S MY KIND OF QUILTING!

VARIATIONS

Add some more echo lines and change out the fillers for a slightly different look.

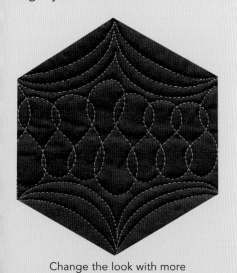

Change the look with more echoes and different fillers.

HEXAGON 1

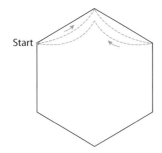

Start

1. Starting from any corner, quilt a line that curves to the next corner and again to the next adjacent corner. Echo the line that you just quilted, returning to the starting point.

TIP

If you are working on a straight row of hexagons, you could repeat Step 1 to quilt all the tops before moving on to the next step.

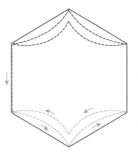

2. Travel down the edge of the block and repeat Step 1, quilting the bottom of the hexagon the same as the top.

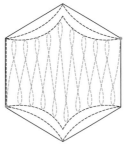

3. Fill the area in between with the filler of your choice.

This design makes a cool secondary pattern when quilted in a group of hexagons.

HEXAGON 2

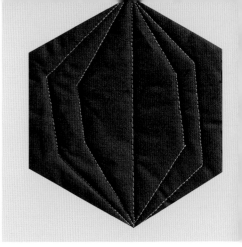

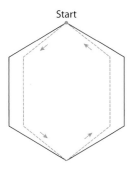
Start

1. From any corner, quilt a diagonal line to about 1″ inside the next corner, then echo the next side of the block and angle back down to the opposite corner from the starting point. Continue stitching to repeat the pattern on the other side of the block.

THIS DESIGN IS A VARIATION OF THE "DOT-TO-DOT" TECHNIQUE, WHICH USES THE CORNERS AND SIDES OF A BLOCK TO CREATE INTRICATE-LOOKING DESIGNS. IT CONSISTS ONLY OF STRAIGHT LINES, SO FEEL FREE TO PULL OUT YOUR WALKING FOOT FOR THIS ONE.

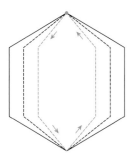

2. Echo inside the quilting lines, coming to a point at the starting and ending corners.

> **TIP**
>
> This design ends directly across from the starting point, making it great for hexagons that are pieced in rows or rings. This means that you can go directly from block to block without traveling or starting a new line of quilting.

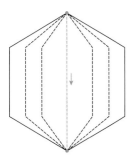

3. Quilt a line straight across to the opposite corner to move on to the next block.

VARIATIONS

Replace the straight line with some free-motion quilting for an easy variation of this design.

Add texture by stitching a free-motion design in the center.

To create a really nice secondary design, echo quilt just one side of the block and free-motion quilt the rest. When the hexagons are arranged in a flower or ring formation and the echo quilting is on the inside edge of each hexagon, the straight lines create a star-like pattern.

Create a star pattern by echo quilting just the inside edge of each hexagon in a ring.

SOMETIMES I WANT CERTAIN BLOCKS TO REALLY STAND OUT, AND THIS DESIGN MAKES THAT HAPPEN. USE IT IN AREAS THAT YOU WANT TO HIGHLIGHT, OR IN THE CENTER OF GROUPS OF HEXAGONS. I LIKE TO START THIS DESIGN IN THE CENTER OF THE BLOCK TO HELP ENSURE THAT IT'S AS SYMMETRICAL AS POSSIBLE.

HEXAGON 3

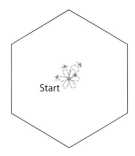

1. Starting in the center of the block, quilt a small flower shape with 6 petals. Try to stitch them so that each loop points to the center of a side.

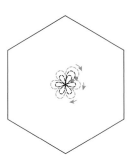

2. Echo around each of the petals, continuing around and around until the outer petals are close to the block sides.

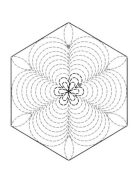

3. To fill in the corners, add a leaf shape on your last time around the petals.

VARIATIONS

For a slight variation, quilt 3 petals instead of 6. Start with the loop of each petal pointing toward a block corner.

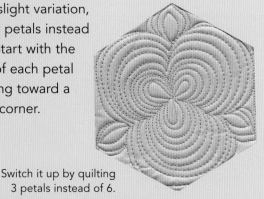

Switch it up by quilting 3 petals instead of 6.

For a different look, stop echoing the petals halfway through and fill in the rest of the space with a different pattern. This is what I do when the design isn't looking as even as I would like.

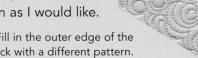

Fill in the outer edge of the block with a different pattern.

HEXAGON 4

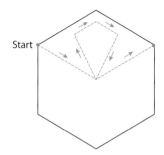 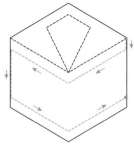 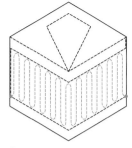

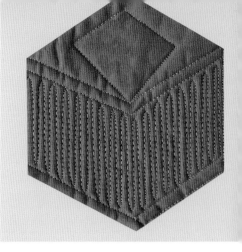

1. Quilt a line that angles down from a corner about 2″. Quilt a diamond-shaped design and then continue on to the next corner.

2. Travel along the edge of the block ¼″ and echo underneath the line from Step 1. Travel along the edge of the block and echo the bottom 2 sides of the hexagon.

3. Quilt the space between the lines with the filler of your choice. In this example, I quilted back-and-forth lines.

THIS DESIGN USES THE CORNERS OF THE BLOCK TO CREATE A DESIGN THAT LOOKS AWESOME WHEN USED IN A ROW OF HEXAGONS. IT WORKS IN A VARIETY OF SIZES AND IS EASY TO CUSTOMIZE TO YOUR PREFERENCES.

VARIATIONS

Create a chevron effect by quilting the design in a straight row of hexagons.

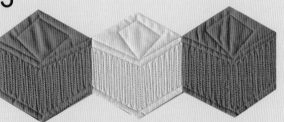

A zigzag pattern emerges in a row of hexagons.

Try changing out the fillers for a fun variation of the design.

Different fillers can alter the density of the design.

When quilting multiple rows, try changing up the direction of the design for a different secondary design.

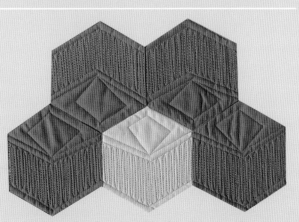

Alternate the placement of the straight lines.

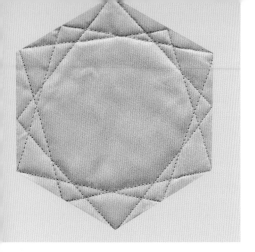

DIAMONDS ARE A QUILTER'S BEST FRIEND, EVEN WHEN THEY ARE PART OF A HEXAGON BLOCK. THIS DESIGN USES THE EDGE OF THE BLOCK AS A REFERENCE POINT, MEANING YOU DON'T HAVE TO MARK THE DESIGN. IT IS FAST AND FUN TO STITCH, MAKING IT ONE OF MY FAVORITES.

HEXAGON 5

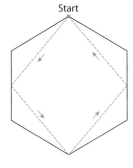

Start

1. From any corner, quilt a line diagonally to the middle of the next side, on to the opposite corner, across to the middle of the next side, and back to the starting point.

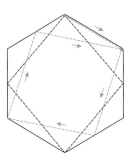

2. Travel along the edge of the block to the next corner and repeat Step 1.

TIP

Once you quilt a few of the lines of this design, it can be hard to figure out where to go next. If you get lost, just pause and take a moment to find the next quilting point.

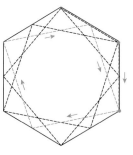

3. Travel along to the next corner and repeat Step 1 again. When you finish, you will have quilted into every corner of the hexagon.

note When you have finished with this design, you will have traveled in the seam of two of the sides. When I am quilting this design on my quilts, I go ahead and finish stitching in the rest of the seams. It not only completes the block but also makes the design end where it started. Of course, you can leave that out if you would like.

VARIATIONS

If straight lines aren't your favorite, try curved lines instead.

Curved lines create a playful star.

Before you stitch the last set of lines, add some filler to the center. This is perfect for larger hexagons.

Add a filler before you stitch the final diamond.

HEXAGON 6

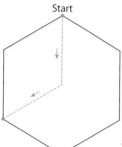

Start

1. Starting from any corner, quilt a diagonal line that stops just short of the middle point of the block. Turn and continue stitching another diagonal line to the second corner from the starting point.

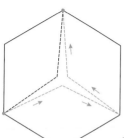

2. Repeat Step 1 twice to divide the block into 3 sections, returning to the starting point.

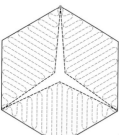

3. Using a back-and-forth line, work your way around the block to fill in all of the small diamonds you have created.

THIS DESIGN SHOWS JUST HOW MUCH I LIKE TO DIVIDE BLOCKS INTO SMALLER PIECES. IT ADDS A DIFFERENT LOOK TO THE BLOCK AND IS EASY TO QUILT WITHOUT MARKING.

VARIATIONS

For smaller hexagons, or for less dense quilting, leave out the filler and throw in a few echo lines instead.

Use echo lines to fill in the diamonds.

This design creates a secondary design when you stitch it in blocks that are in rows. Experiment with different fillers for a new look.

Stitch the same design in a row to create a secondary pattern.

THIS QUICK AND EASY DESIGN MIGHT LOOK FAMILIAR. I LOVE TO USE IT IN BLOCKS OF ALL SHAPES! THE WEDGES FILL IN THE AREA SO WELL, AND IT IS EASY TO STITCH. WHETHER YOUR BLOCKS ARE LARGE OR SMALL, THIS IS A DESIGN THAT YOU ARE JUST GOING TO LOVE TO QUILT.

VARIATIONS

Not only is this design quick and easy, but it looks great when quilted in groups of hexagons.

Radiate the wedge placement in pairs of hexagons to create a frame for a center hexagon.

You can also change up the shape and the number of wedges within the block.

Vary the number of wedges for a slightly different look.

HEXAGON 7

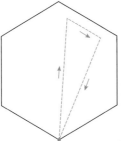

Start

1. From any corner, quilt a line that stops about ¼″ from the opposite corner. Echo one side the block and quilt a diagonal line back to the starting point.

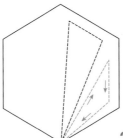

2. Quilt another wedge next the first one, filling the space as completely as possible.

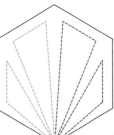

3. Repeat on the other half of the hexagon, quilting the same number of wedges.

note I like to quilt half of the block and then the other half. It helps keep the design symmetrical without requiring the time to mark it!

HEXAGON 8

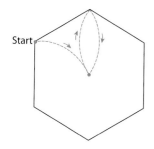

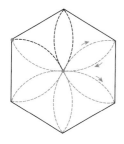

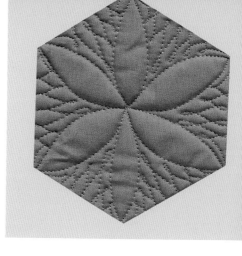

1. Starting from any corner, quilt a line that arcs to the center of the block, up to the next corner, and back to the center.

THIS DESIGN COMBINES A BASIC CONTINUOUS CURVE WITH A FILLER TO CREATE A MORE COMPLEX-LOOKING DESIGN. USE THIS IN AREAS OF THE QUILT THAT YOU WANT TO SHINE. IT WILL DEFINITELY GET ATTENTION!

2. Continue quilting your way around the block, arcing to each corner and back to the center, until you return to the starting point.

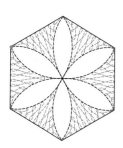

3. Fill in the spaces between the edge of the block and the quilting with the design of your choice, working your way around the block until you return to the starting point.

VARIATIONS

Try using this design in blocks of several different shapes, such as squares.

TIP

If you are quilting a large block or working with a smaller sewing machine, you can quilt the design in a different order to make it easier.

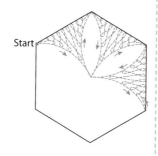

Quilt half of the block with curved lines, and then fill in the top, returning to the starting point.

Repeat with the bottom half of the block.

Try the design in other shapes, such as this 4-petal pattern in a square.

THIS DESIGN USES THE CORNERS OF THE BLOCK TO MAKE AN INTRICATE DESIGN. IT MAY SEEM A LITTLE COMPLEX AT FIRST GLANCE, BUT IT'S JUST A COUPLE OF STEPS REPEATED TWICE. LIKE MOST OF THE OTHER DESIGNS IN THIS SECTION, IT LOOKS GREAT IN MULTIPLE BLOCKS.

VARIATIONS

Since you create diamonds and triangles in Steps 1 and 2, you can change up this design

Echo the lines for a more complex look.

by filling them in with different patterns. Or just add more echo lines to the design for a more complex look to your blocks.

Experiment with differently shaped blocks, including squares.

This pattern looks great quilted in a square.

HEXAGON 9

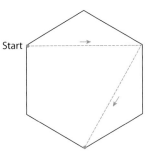

Start

1. From any corner, quilt a horizontal line to the second corner from the starting point, then diagonally to the second corner away from that point.

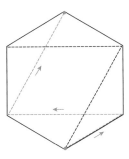

2. Travel back along the edge of the block to the corner between the last 2 points. Repeat Step 1 on the other side of the block.

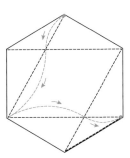

3. Follow the straight lines you stitched in Steps 1 and 2 to add curved lines to the design. Quilt a curved line from the last corner to the intersection of the straight lines, then change the direction of the curve as you stitch to the next corner. Repeat to work your way to the opposite side of the block.

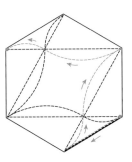

4. Travel back along the edge of the block to the next corner and repeat Step 3 to quilt the other side.

HEXAGON 10

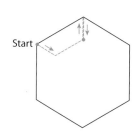

1. From any corner, quilt a 2″ diagonal line. Turn and echo the side of the block, stopping about 2″ away from the next corner. Quilt a line up to the corner, then travel back to the last point.

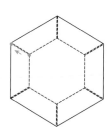

2. Work your way around the block, echoing each side until you end up about 2″ from the starting corner.

THIS IS A SIMPLE DESIGN THAT GIVES THE BLOCK AN ELEGANT LOOK, ALMOST LIKE A JEWEL. IT'S A DESIGN THAT I LIKE TO USE WHEN I WANT TO SHOW OFF THE FABRIC IN THE BLOCK, OR IF I WANT LIGHT QUILTING FOR ANY REASON.

CHECK OUT HOW EYE-CATCHING THIS DESIGN IS WHEN USED IN MULTIPLE BLOCKS.

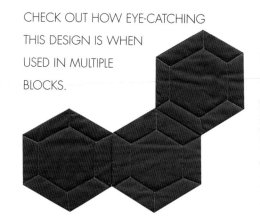

3. Travel along the first line you quilted in Step 1 to return to the starting point.

VARIATIONS

Before you stitch Step 3, quilt the inner hexagon with a different design.

Add filler quilting to the inner hexagon.

If you don't like traveling along previously stitched lines, leave out every other travel line. You still have an interesting design with half the work.

Omit every other short line between the inner hexagon and the edge of the block.

If you really want to show off your quilting skills, you can quilt it again.

Stitch another hexagon inside the first.

section 2:
BACKGROUND FILLERS

STARBURST 86

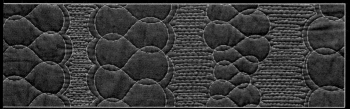

RIBBON ROWS 88

OFFSET SQUARES 90

PEBBLED LEAVES 92

WAVY SERPENTINE LINES 94

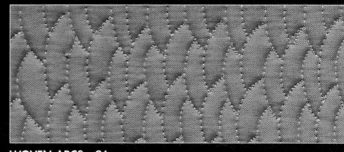

WOVEN ARCS 96

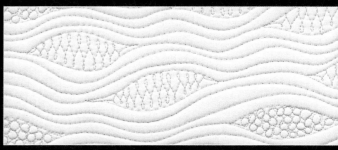

WOODGRAIN VARIATION 98

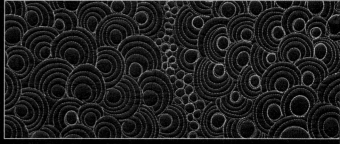

ECHOED PEBBLES 100

PAISLEY FEATHER 102

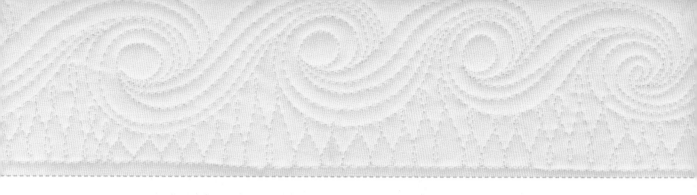

Laurel, designed, pieced, and quilted by Angela Walters

Why Fillers Are So Handy

It is fun to learn a lot of quilting designs, but honestly, just knowing a few good background filler designs will get you started. In this section, I show you how to quilt several different designs that will work well in different areas of your quilt.

Other Ways to Use Filler Designs

Background filler designs are patterns that work well around other elements of a quilt—for instance, around blocks or other quilting motifs. But the great thing about background filler designs is that you can use them in a few different ways as well.

Use as Allover Designs

Instead of limiting these designs to backgrounds of your quilt, you can use them all over your quilt. This is especially helpful for quilts that you need to finish quickly!

Combine Designs

If you can't choose a single design for your quilt, try combining two fillers for a different look. For example, you could combine Pebbled Leaves (page 92) with the Starburst Filler (page 86) for quilting that helps add extra detail to your quilt.

With a bit of planning, a combination of fillers will flow gracefully from one to the next.

Tips for Improving Meanders

Meanders or filler designs can be a little challenging, especially when it comes to quilting consistently over the whole quilt. These tips will help make the quilting process a little easier.

▶ DRAW, DRAW, DRAW.

If you have read any of my previous books, you know that I am an advocate for drawing out designs before you sew. Even though the quilting movement is different from drawing, drawing helps your brain learn where to go next. According to a study that I just made up, 80 percent of quilting is knowing where to go next! After you can draw the design, translating it to the quilting machine is all you have left to learn.

▶ JUST THROW SOMETHING IN.

When it comes to actually quilting the designs, let me encourage you to not worry about quilting perfectly. Instead, focus on filling in spaces as consistently as possible. My theory is that a gap in the quilting is more noticeable than an error in the individual design.

Don't Be Too Hard on Yourself

While quilting, it can be easy to start critiquing the job that you are doing while you are doing it. Try not to let that inner voice talk too loudly. After you are finished, and the quilt isn't 2″ away from your nose, I think you will notice that the quilting looks better than you thought it would.

Ready?

Let's learn some fun background fillers to use on your next quilt.

THIS DESIGN WORKS FROM SIDE TO SIDE AND IS EASY TO STITCH FREE-HAND, WITH NO NEED TO MARK. YOU CAN CHANGE THE DENSITY OF THE DESIGN BY MAKING THE LINES CLOSER TOGETHER OR FARTHER APART. THE STARBURST DESIGN WORKS IN AREAS OF ANY SIZE, EVEN INSIDE BLOCKS.

TIP

Even though I am demonstrating this design working down the quilt, you could do it in any direction. Try quilting it from the bottom up, or in a horizontal direction going from side to side.

STARBURST

Start

1. Starting from either side, quilt a straight line for a couple of inches. Stop and quilt a star, or asterisk shape, by quilting up a vertical line that extends above and below your straight line, returning to the middle. Add 2 diagonal lines in alternate directions, with all lines meeting in the center.

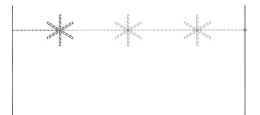

2. Continue quilting your way across the area by alternating between straight lines and stars until you reach the other edge.

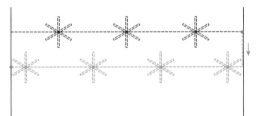

3. Travel up or down ½˝ along the edge of the quilting area (whether it's a seam or the edge of the quilt) and quilt back in the opposite direction. Stagger the placement of the stars so they fall between the stars in the previous row.

note Offsetting your stars will help the lines fit closer together and will make your quilting more dense.

VARIATIONS

Want a different look? Here are a couple of fun-to-stitch variations.

Quilt just the tops of each star for a grassy look that's especially great for landscape or art quilts.

Create a grassy look by quilting only the tops of the stars.

Make it a meander. Instead of quilting in straight rows, change directions as you stitch. This is especially helpful if you are quilting on a sewing machine because you can work in sections instead of straight across the quilt.

Make the lines meander across the quilt.

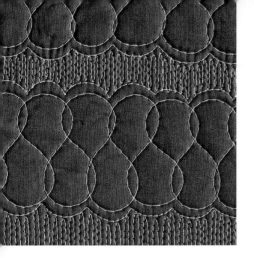

THE CLASSIC RIBBON CANDY DESIGN IS PERFECT FOR NARROW BORDERS AND SASHING AND IS ONE OF MY FAVORITE DESIGNS. QUILTING THE RIBBON CANDY DESIGN SO THAT IT OVERLAPS RESULTS IN A FUN DESIGN PERFECT FOR LARGER AREAS OF BACKGROUND SPACE. IT REALLY MOVES YOUR EYE ACROSS THE QUILT.

note

To quilt the classic ribbon candy design, quilt a line that curves out and back, almost like a backward S shape. Without stopping, curve away from the S and back to touch the first curve you quilted.

If you have a hard time getting the shape right, try drawing it until you become familiar with the process.

RIBBON ROWS

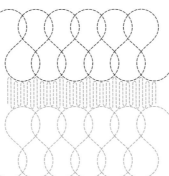

1. Quilt the ribbon candy design across the quilting area, overlapping the curves by about ¼˝.

2. Quilt another row of overlapping ribbon candy a couple of inches below the first. Fill in the space between the rows with a filler, such as a back-and-forth line.

TIP

If you don't want the individual rows of ribbon candy to stand out as much, use a swirly filler or something similar to the ribbon candy. This helps them blend in a little more, which is handy if you aren't happy with the way they turned out.

To blend the rows, use a swirly filler instead of the up-and-down lines.

VARIATIONS

Once you learn this design, it's easy to come up with some interesting variations.

Alternate between taller and shorter curves to create a design that looks much harder than it actually is.

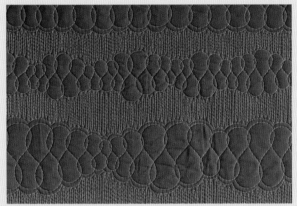

Vary the size of the curves to make a complex-looking design.

Don't worry about marking the lines. Instead, aim for symmetry. For instance, alternate between 2 taller loops and 3 shorter loops. It will look nice and even, and you won't have had to spend time marking them.

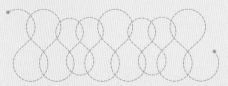

Vary the height of the loops, aiming for symmetry.

Instead of alternating between different sizes, you can quilt a row so that it grows bigger or smaller.

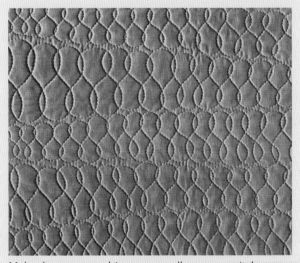

Make the row grow bigger or smaller as you stitch.

You can adapt this design for the larger borders of your quilt. Just quilt a row down the center and quilt a filler design on either side. It's quick and stunning!

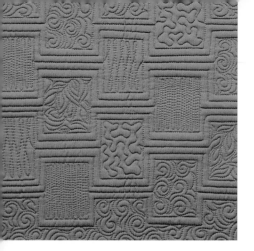

THIS DESIGN IS A VARIATION OF THE SQUARE-CHAIN DESIGN THAT YOU MAY HAVE SEEN IN MY OTHER BOOK, *SHAPE BY SHAPE FREE-MOTION QUILTING WITH ANGELA WALTERS.* IT COMBINES FREE-MOTION QUILTING AND STRAIGHT LINES TO CREATE AN IMPACTFUL DESIGN.

TIP

It may be tempting to pull out the ruler or walking foot to quilt the straight lines, but try quilting it without them. Once the entire area is filled in, all you will see is the overall texture of the design.

OFFSET SQUARES

Start

1. Starting from any side of the quilt, stitch a box by quilting a line that goes up, across, down, back, and up to the starting point. It doesn't matter what size you make the square, but I tend to make mine about 3″–4″.

2. Fill inside the box with a free-motion quilting design of your choice, working your way to the midpoint of the opposite side of the box. For this example, I used a wishbone design.

TIP

It doesn't matter what kind of design you use—just that you end up on the opposite side from where you started.

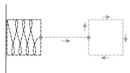

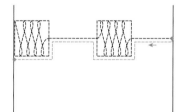

3. Quilt a straight line about the length of the first box. Quilt another box the same size as the first.

4. Continue quilting across the area by quilting squares and straight lines. Travel down the edge of the quilting area about ½″ and echo your way around the boxes and straight lines, back to the starting point.

note The echoing may seem like an unnecessary step, but it helps separate the boxes and enhances the look of the design.

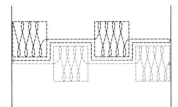

5. Stitch the next row by quilting a straight line under the boxes of the previous row and quilting boxes in gaps. The result is a set of rows that interlock with each other and give a custom look to the quilt.

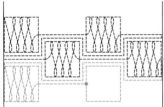

6. Continue quilting rows of boxes and echo lines until you get to the edge of the quilting area.

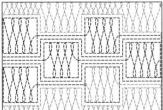

7. At the top and bottom of the quilting area, you will have some small, unquilted spaces. Just fill in around them with more echo lines and the same filler you used inside the boxes.

TIP

What if your squares are more like rectangles? Don't worry about it! As long as the area is filled in, it will look great.

VARIATIONS

Mix it up! Instead of quilting the same free-motion design in all the squares, choose a few and alternate between them. It's a great way to practice new designs or to showcase your favorites.

Quilt a different filler in each square or rectangle.

Or, you can alternate between rows of regular squares and free-motion quilting designs.

Alternate between curvy and straight-line fillers.

No matter how you mix it up, it will look great!

DO YOU WANT A DESIGN WITH A LOT OF TEXTURE AND CONTRAST? THEN THE PEBBLED LEAVES DESIGN IS PERFECT FOR YOU. WHETHER YOU PLACE THE LEAVES STRATEGICALLY IN YOUR QUILT OR USE THEM IN AN ALL-OVER DESIGN, I AM SURE THAT YOU WILL BE PLEASED WITH THE RESULT

note This is a great way to practice quilting pebbles without committing to using them over the whole quilt. Try stitching a few. If you decide that you don't like quilting them, switch to regular leaves.

PEBBLED LEAVES

1. Quilt a leaf shape by quilting a curve that arcs out to a point and returns to the starting point. Make the shape 2″ or bigger so that you don't have to squeeze the pebbles into a small area.

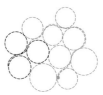

2. Fill the shape by quilting pebbles, ending at the original starting point.

TIP

To quilt the pebble shape:

1. Start by quilting a circle.

2. Quilt the next circle in the opposite direction of the first. This is what helps them stick together. Quilt another circle.

3. Continue working your way around the area, quilting circle shapes to fill in the area as consistently as possible.

---

3. Echo around the outside of the leaf shape. It doesn't matter how many times you echo; the echoing just helps separate the pebbles from the rest of the quilting, making them stand out a bit more.

4. Start the next leaf by pointing the arc shape in a different direction than the first leaf.

5. Continue adding leaves and filling in with pebbles as you move around the quilting area, filling in as consistently as possible.

note Stuck? If you are having trouble with your leafy meander, try these tips:

▪ Use echoing to help move around the area. You can echo what you have just quilted or leaves that you quilted previously.

▪ Try to make your leaves point in many different directions (unless, of course, you want them all facing the same way). This will help make them look more like an allover design.

▪ If you have any awkwardly shaped areas, just throw in a few more pebbles.

VARIATIONS

This design is stunning but can be time-consuming to stitch. If you don't have time to stitch it in a big filler area or just want to add a bit of interest to your quilt instead, use the pebbled leaves as a way to frame a special quilt block.

You can also quilt the leaves so that they add detail to other quilt blocks. In this example, I quilted leaves between quilt blocks.

Frame a quilt block with Pebble Leaves.

Note how the leaf shapes create a glow around the star block.

Or if you like pebbles, you can quilt more of them with leaves thrown in.

Quilt lots of pebbles with a few leaves.

THIS DESIGN HAS AN AMAZING TEX-
TURE THAT RESULTS FROM COMBINING
WAVY LINES AND SERPENTINE LINES.
IT ESPECIALLY LOOKS GREAT WHEN
QUILTED WITH A THREAD COLOR
THAT MATCHES THE QUILT TOP.

WAVY SERPENTINE LINES

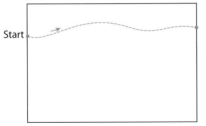
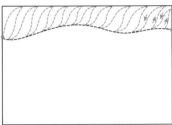

1. Quilt a gently waving line from one side of the quilting area to the opposite side.

2. Fill above the wavy line by quilting an S-shaped serpentine line, working your way back to the starting point.

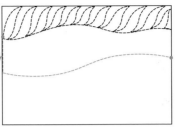

3. Travel along the side of the quilting area a couple of inches and quilt another wavy line to the opposite side.

note Don't worry about making the wavy lines echo each other. In fact, I think that this design looks best when the wavy lines are slightly off-kilter and completely different.

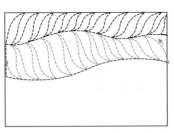
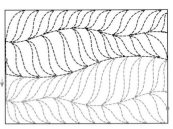

4. Fill above the wavy line with a serpentine line, just as you did in Step 2. Because I am easily amused, I thought it would be fun to stitch my serpentine lines in different directions.

5. Continue working your way down the quilting area, quilting wavy lines and filling in above them.

VARIATIONS

Once you have the basic idea of this design, you can experiment with the placement of the wavy lines.

If the serpentine lines are giving you trouble, try a basic arc as a filler or use any kind of filler that you would like.

Replace the serpentine lines with arc shapes for an easy-to-stitch design.

You could also use a different filler in every other row.

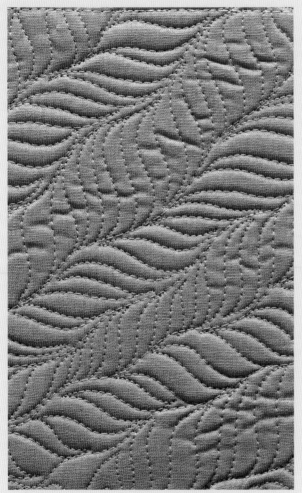

Quilt the serpentine lines at diagonal angles or in other directions.

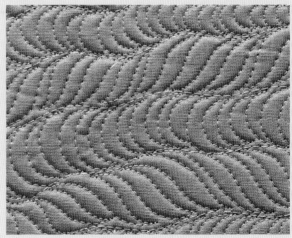

Alternate between fillers to add interest.

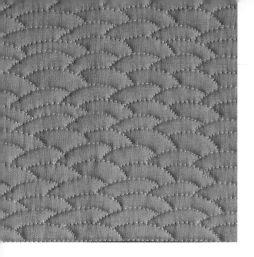

WOVEN ARCS

THIS FILLER IS SMALLER AND HAS A WOVEN LOOK TO IT. IT TAKES THE CLASSIC DESIGN, SHRINKS IT DOWN, AND ADDS A BIT OF TRAVEL FOR A DESIGN THAT IS BIG ON TEXTURE.

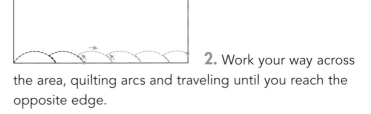

1. Starting at a lower corner of the quilting area, stitch a small arc, then travel back along the curve for about ¼″. Quilt another arc.

2. Work your way across the area, quilting arcs and traveling until you reach the opposite edge.

3. Travel up along the edge of the quilting area about ¼″, then echo the arc quilted underneath it. Travel back along the edge of the arc about ¼″ and quilt another arc.

4. Continue quilting the second row of arcs until you reach the opposite side.

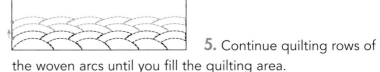

5. Continue quilting rows of the woven arcs until you fill the quilting area.

TIP

For this particular design, I like to keep my arc fairly small.

VARIATIONS

Don't limit the design to background quilting. Try it in borders for a striking effect.

As an alternative to straight lines, quilt the arcs so that they wrap around an element, such as a row of larger pebbles.

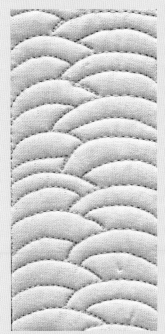

Stitch a narrow section of quilted arcs in a border.

Note how the arcs frame this row of pebbles.

You could also quilt these a lot larger and fill in between the lines for a more complex-looking design.

Quilt the first arc slightly larger and then quilt a filler design, working your way back to the starting point. Echo around the shape. Travel back along the previously quilted echo line and quilt the next arc.

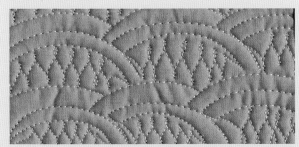

These Woven Arcs look lacy when enlarged and filled with Double Wishbones (page 114).

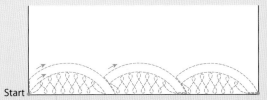

You can quilt larger arcs and fill them with a contrasting dense design.

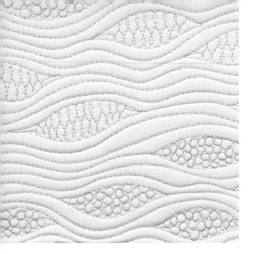

WOODGRAIN VARIATION

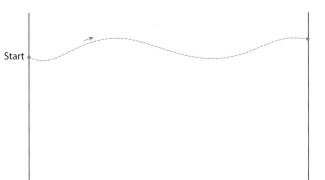

THIS DESIGN COMBINES FREE-MOTION QUILTING WITH THE WOODGRAIN DESIGN FOR A DIFFERENT LOOK.

1. Quilt a gently waving line from one side of the quilting area to the opposite side.

TIPS

A few tips to help you get the best-looking design:

▪ To avoid gaps in the quilting, quilt the pod shapes close to the wavy lines.

▪ Space the wavy lines as consistently as possible. Quilting small or inconsistent waves will make it harder to echo and even harder to fit the pod shapes.

▪ If any areas do not fit together well, just quilt some filler designs inside the area to help the design look more consistent.

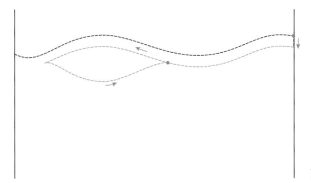

2. Travel down along the edge about ½˝ and begin echoing the line that you just quilted. At a random point, stop and quilt a pod shape that arcs back and touches the line you are quilting.

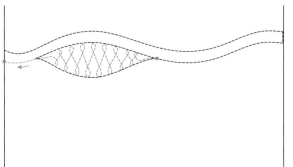

3. Fill in the pod with the free-motion quilting design of your choice, working your way to the opposite side. Continue echoing the wavy line.

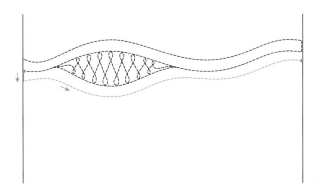

4. Travel down along the edge of the quilt and echo the waving line back to the other side.

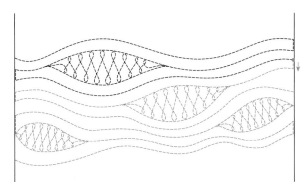

5. Continue quilting wavy lines, adding filled pods in random areas.

VARIATIONS

Alternate between a few of your favorite filler designs. It's a great way to practice a few new-to-you quilting designs.

I tend to quilt the pod shapes so that they are fairly small and compact. However, you can experiment with different sizes from teeny to large. Find a style that fits your preferences.

Try filling in the pods with different designs.

ECHOED PEBBLES

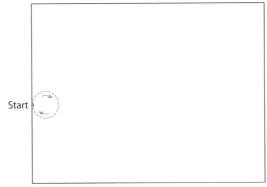

ECHOED PEBBLES CAN REALLY HIGH-
LIGHT AREAS OF YOUR QUILT. MAKE THE
PEBBLES AS LARGE OR AS SMALL AS YOU
LIKE TO FIT THE SCALE OF YOUR QUILT.

1. Quilt a circle
shape that touches the edge of a block.

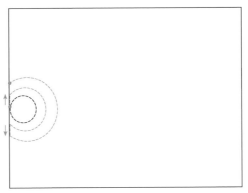

TIP

It doesn't matter how many
times you echo around the
circle. Add as many echoes
as you wish!

2. Travel along
the edge of the block about ¼″ and echo around the circle
until you reach the other side. Travel along the edge of the
block and echo again.

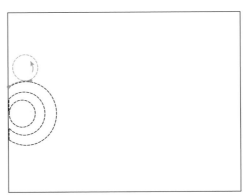

3. Travel along
the last echo line about ¼″ and quilt another circle.

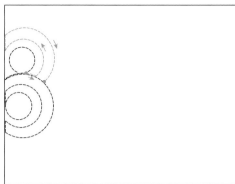

4. Travel and add a few echoes, just as you did on the first pebble.

5. Continue adding pebbles and echo lines until the area is completely filled in.

VARIATIONS

Quilted pebbles require some traveling around the original circle. You could smooth out the travel lines and highlight the circles by stitching around each at least twice before starting the echo lines.

Add a defined look to each pebble by stitching around it a few times before echoing.

Since this is a variation of a pebble, you can combine it with regular pebbles for a different look.

Draw attention to part of the quilt by inserting some regular pebbles.

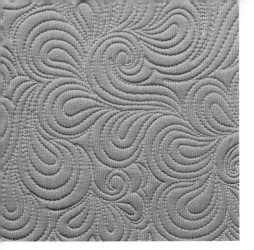

I LOVE FEATHERS AND I LOVE ECHOING, SO IT MAKES PERFECT SENSE THAT I WOULD INCLUDE A DESIGN THAT CONTAINS BOTH! THIS DESIGN IS PERFECT FOR QUILT BACKGROUNDS BECAUSE YOU CAN MAKE THE MOTIFS AS LARGE OR AS SMALL AS YOU WOULD LIKE. IT ALSO ADDS A BEAUTIFUL TEXTURE TO YOUR QUILT.

PAISLEY FEATHER

1. Quilt an elongated swirl and echo back to the starting point. Echo it twice more, ending at the same place you started.

2. At the bottom of the swirl, quilt a paisley that extends away from the swirl.

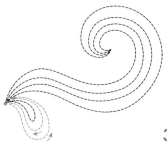

3. Echo around the paisley at least twice.

4. Add another paisley between the first paisley and the swirl.

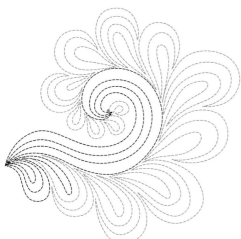

5. Echo around the new paisley. Continue working your way around the swirl by quilting paisleys and echoing around them. As you work inside the swirl, the paisleys will become smaller.

6. To begin the next paisley feather, echo around the paisleys until you reach the point where you want to add the next one. Quilt an elongated swirl and continue quilting.

TIPS
Beautiful Paisley Feathers

▪ Don't be afraid to echo. Echoing around the paisleys is what really makes this design shine. Echoing also helps hide any mistakes. So, when in doubt … echo!

▪ If you have any spaces that are too small for a paisley feather, just add some paisleys by themselves. Or you can add a different design, such as pebbles.

Add single paisleys or pebbles to fill in small spaces.

▪ Keep your paisleys skinny, almost like a finger. That will give you space to add more echoing around it.

▪ Oh, and don't forget to echo. I know I have already said that, but it's important to remember!

section 3:
BORDERS

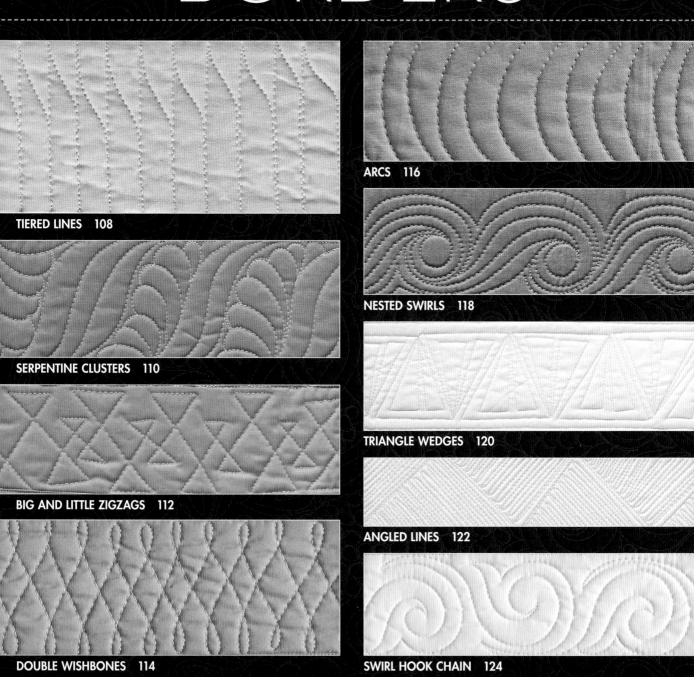

Oh, borders—I tend to have a love-hate relationship with them. Honestly, this is the area of a quilt that is probably my least favorite to quilt! But over the years, I have learned how to manage them and make the process a little easier.

Pieced by Ruth Doss and quilted by Angela Walters

About This Chapter

In this section, you will learn several different designs, including some attractive variations, for borders of all sizes. I will also show you how to turn the corners of each design, since that can be the trickiest part. My hope is that after reading this section, you will like quilting borders even more than I do.

Turning the Corner

When it comes to wrapping the designs around the corner of the border I have a couple of go-to options.

▶ USE A PIVOT POINT.

My favorite way of turning the corner uses the inner border corner as a pivot point. Having this point as a reference will help you visualize the turn and wrap it around the corner.

▶ SWITCH IT UP.

Some designs, including a few in this chapter, don't turn the corner very easily. In those cases, I use a different design altogether in the border corner.

Stitch a different design in the border corner.

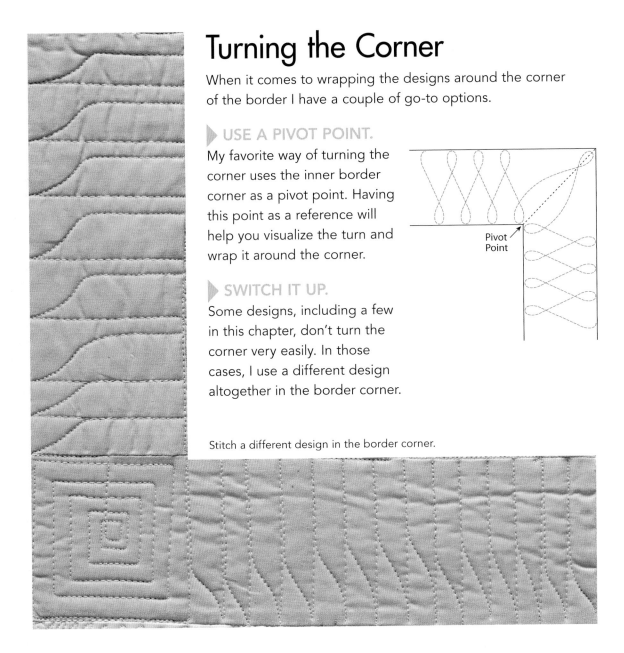

Pivot Point

Making Borders More Manageable

If you are still a little hesitant to work on the borders of your quilt, here are a couple of easy options.

▶ MAKE THE CORNERS SPECIAL.

Instead of working your way all around the border, you could add a design in the corners, then switch to an allover design in the rest of the border. I love this option because it gives the quilt a custom look but is still easy to stitch! At least it's easier than trying to quilt a continuous design down the entire length of the quilt.

▶ USE SIMILAR DESIGNS.

Choosing filler and border designs that are similar will ensure that you don't have to switch between completely different designs.

For example, if I opted to use a feather design in the border, I could choose to use a feather meander in the center of the quilt.

note Choose a stitching direction that works best for you. I show designs moving from left to right, mostly because I work on a longarm machine and the horizontal direction comes naturally to me. Also, the horizontal orientation works better in a book format. However, the designs can be quilted in a different direction, depending on the type of machine you use and the orientation of the quilt.

TIERED LINES

THIS DESIGN COMBINES STRAIGHT LINES AND A GENTLE CURVE TO GIVE THE BORDERS OF YOUR QUILT A SIMPLE, YET INTERESTING, LOOK. IT WORKS IN BORDERS OF ALL WIDTHS AND IS QUICK AND EASY TO DO. THERE IS A LITTLE BIT OF BACKTRACKING OR TRAVELING ON THIS DESIGN, BUT IT'S WELL WORTH THE EXTRA WORK!

note When I stitch this design, I don't worry about marking out the spacing. Instead, I eyeball it and try to keep it as consistent as possible. If the thought of just winging it makes you a little nervous, try marking reference points to help you with the spacing.

Start

1. Quilt a line from a long side of the border to the opposite side. Quilt your way back to the first side by curving away and then straightening out the line to end about ½˝ from the starting point.

2. Quilt a line up to the other side, traveling over part of the line in Step 1.

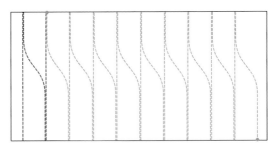

3. Continue quilting straight lines and curves, working your way across the border.

VARIATIONS

If you don't want to travel along the previously stitched lines, you could travel along the bottom of the border ¼˝ or so, then begin the next one.

This makes for less traveling and also spaces them out just a bit.

Leave a little space between each set of lines by traveling along the bottom of the border.

You can easily add a different look to this design by changing the direction or height of the curves.

Vary the height of the curves.

Turning the Corner

This design doesn't pivot easily around the border corner. Instead of trying to make it fit, I quilt a square design in the border corner, then move on to the other side.

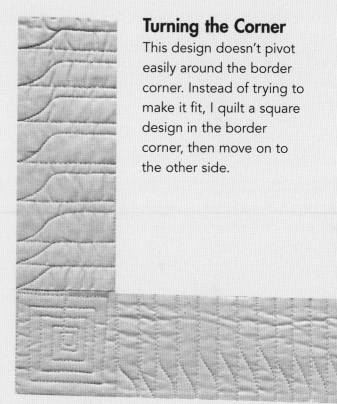

Quilt a design like this square spiral in the border corners.

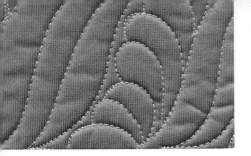

SERPENTINE CLUSTERS

ONE DESIGN THAT I LOVE, LOVE, LOVE TO USE IN BORDERS IS THE SERPENTINE LINE. IT ADDS A BIT OF DEPTH TO THE QUILT BUT IS A QUICK DESIGN TO QUILT (ONCE YOU GET THE HANG OF IT!). THIS VARIATION OF THE SERPENTINE LINE ADDS FREE-MOTION QUILTING MOTIFS FOR AN UNUSUAL LOOK.

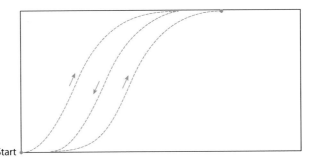

Start

1. Quilt a serpentine line that goes from a long side of the border to the opposite side. Travel along the border edge and echo the line 2 more times.

note When I teach this design in classes, some quilters have trouble getting the hang of changing directions. If you are having trouble, practice drawing the lines a few times to get a feel for the flow of the design.

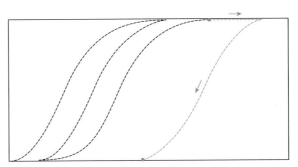

2. After quilting a group of serpentine lines, travel along the edge of the border for about 2″ and quilt another serpentine line.

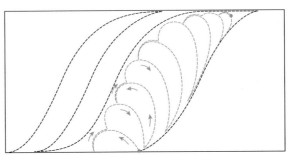

3. Before continuing with the serpentine lines, fill the gap with a different design. I quilted the sides of a feather, but you could quilt something different, such as a wishbone design.

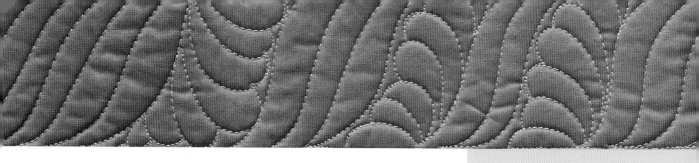

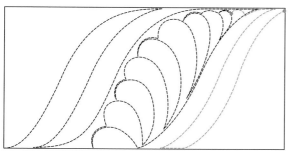

4. Continue quilting the design across the border, alternating between groups of serpentine lines and a filler design.

5. When you get the corner of the border, quilt the lines so that they wrap around to the next side.

note Even though I tend to quilt the serpentine lines in groups of three, you could have more or fewer lines in your group.

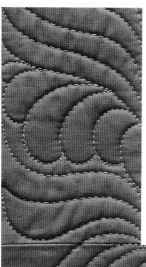

Use the inner border corner as a reference to wrap the serpentine lines around the corner.

VARIATIONS

Switch up the design to make it work for you!

Instead of quilting all the serpentine lines in the same direction, you can alternate between directions to create a different texture. This gives the design a different look altogether.

Change the direction of every other set of lines to create a more open look.

Try experimenting with different fillers to find which one works best for you.

This wishbone filler makes the serpentine lines stand out more.

BIG AND LITTLE ZIGZAGS

THIS ZIGZAG DESIGN VARIATION IS A PERFECT EXAMPLE OF HOW CHANGING THE SCALE OF A DESIGN CAN RESULT IN AN EYE-CATCHING NEW OPTION FOR YOUR QUILT.

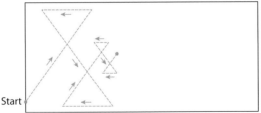

Start

1. Starting about ¼″ from a long side of the border, quilt a diagonal line up toward the opposite side, stopping about ¼″ from the seam. Echo back along the side of the border about 1″ and then angle down toward the starting side. Echo back about 1″, then quilt a diagonal line up past the center of the border. Repeat the triangle shape, making it smaller than the first one.

note The classic zigzag design looks like a wishbone with pointy edges.

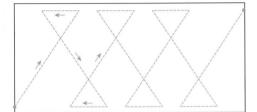

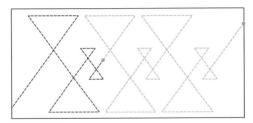

2. Continue quilting the design, alternating between large and small triangles.

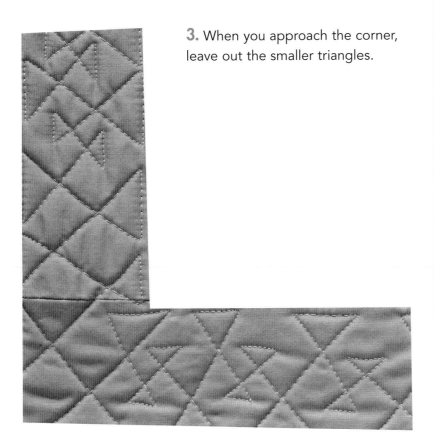

3. When you approach the corner, leave out the smaller triangles.

VARIATIONS

To add a soft look to the design, switch out the small triangle shapes with a wishbone. So easy and fun!

You can stitch wishbones instead of small triangles for a softer look.

Or, if changing sizes is difficult for you, try just alternating between a wishbone and a triangle.

Alternate straight lines and curves by stitching a full-size wishbone between every set of triangles.

DOUBLE WISHBONES

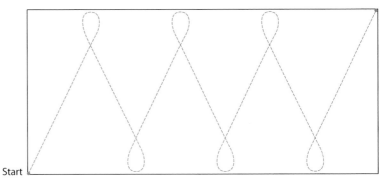

WHAT'S BETTER THAN QUILTING THE WISHBONE DESIGN IN YOUR NARROW BORDERS AND SASHING? TWICE THE WISHBONES! THIS DESIGN SPREADS OUT THE BASIC WISHBONE DESIGN AND FILLS IN WITH A SECOND ONE.

Start

1. Starting on a long side of the border, quilt a wishbone design across the border. Spread the wishbones out about 1″ or so to leave room for the next step.

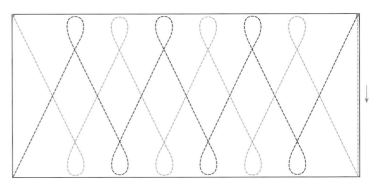

2. Work your way back across the border, quilting new wishbones between those you stitched in Step 1.

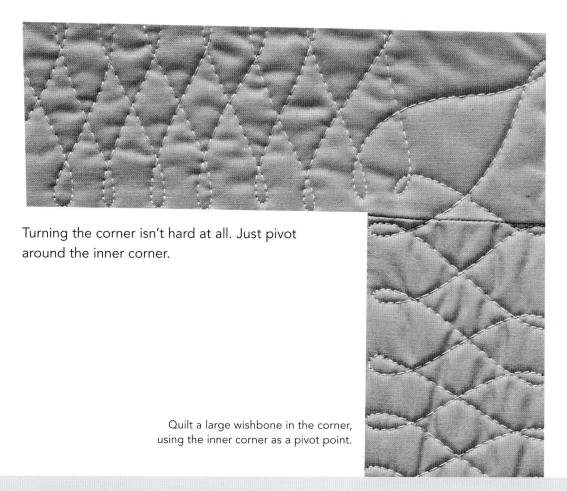

Turning the corner isn't hard at all. Just pivot around the inner corner.

Quilt a large wishbone in the corner, using the inner corner as a pivot point.

VARIATION

Make a softer, rounder wishbone design by placing the circles inside the curved lines.

Alter the entire look of the wishbone design by changing the placement of the circles.

ARCS

THE ARC DESIGN IS A BASIC BUT VERY USEFUL DESIGN. WHEN I WORK ON A QUILT WITH SEVERAL NARROW BORDERS, THIS IS MY GO-TO DESIGN. I ALSO LIKE TO USE IT IN RECTANGLE AND WEDGE BLOCKS.

note In outer borders, stop at least ¼″ from the edge to keep the design from getting lost under the binding.

1. Starting from a long side of the border, quilt a line that gently curves to the other side. Try to land directly across from the starting point, but don't stress out about it.

2. Travel about ½″ along the edge of the border and echo the curve back to the starting side. If you prefer, you could quilt the lines ¼″ apart for a denser design.

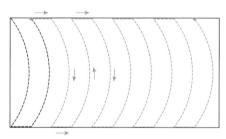

3. Continue quilting along the border, alternating between traveling and echoing.

4. To turn the corner, use the inner corner as the pivot point. The spacing of the arcs will be a little wider toward the outside of your border.

Radiate the curves from the inner corner as you pivot around the border corner.

VARIATIONS

The original design has a gentle curve; you can really exaggerate the curve if you like the different look.

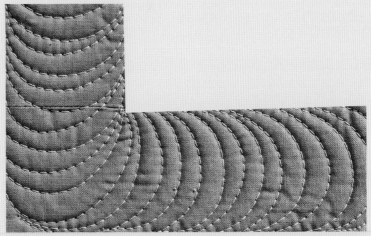

Make the curve deeper for a denser look.

For a simple way to create contrast between several small borders or sashing, quilt a border of curved lines next to a border of straight lines.

Stitch a border of arcs between 2 borders of straight lines.

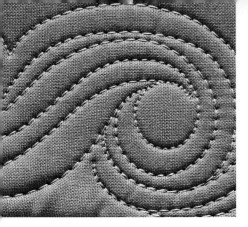

THIS DESIGN MAY LOOK COMPLEX, BUT IT'S MOSTLY ECHOING. ONCE YOU GET THE HANG OF IT, YOU WILL BE SURPRISED AT HOW QUICKLY YOU WILL BE ABLE TO QUILT THE BORDERS OF YOUR QUILT!

NESTED SWIRLS

1. In the middle of the border, quilt a circle that moves into an S-shaped line and ends in another circle.

note Try to stitch the circles in the middle of the border to keep the design even on both sides.

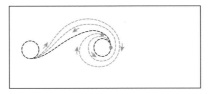

2. Echo around the outside of the line, tucking the end of the line into the first circle. Echo back around to the second circle.

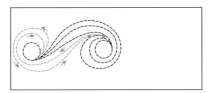

3. Repeat on the inside of the swirl line, echoing to the first circle and back again.

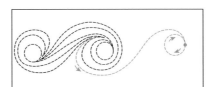

4. Continue by quilting another S-shaped line ending in a circle. Try to keep the circles evenly spaced out, but don't worry too much about it. The echoing around the design will add to the overall texture.

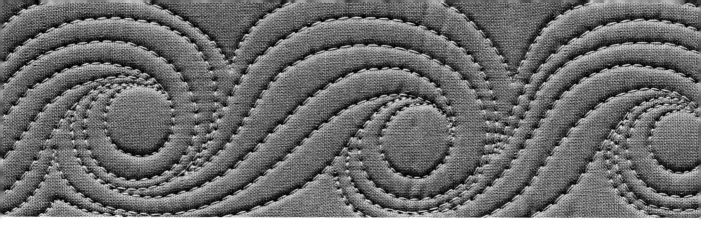

5. Repeat Steps 2 and 3 to echo the line. Continue adding more echoed S lines and circles to fill the border.

TIP

For wide borders, add more echo lines to help fill in the spaces consistently. Or try some other fillers around the swirled line.

Add echo lines or other fillers around the swirls to fill in space on large borders.

You could also add some paisley shapes as well.

Small paisleys are a charming way to fill in the space.

6. To quilt around the corner, end an S line with a circle in the center of the corner. Echo around the shape as usual, then stitch the next S line in a perpendicular direction to continue quilting the next side.

Wrap the design around the border corner by changing the direction of the new S line.

VARIATION

For an allover design, quilt this design in rows and fill between them with another design to create a fun, multilayered look.

Make an unusual background filler by quilting the swirls in rows.

TRIANGLE WEDGES

THIS GEOMETRIC DESIGN IS PERFECT FOR GRAPHIC, MODERN QUILTS. YOU ALSO CAN TRY IT ON LARGE BORDERS OF ALL KINDS. IT MAY LOOK COMPLEX, BUT IT'S ACTUALLY PRETTY EASY ONCE YOU GET THE HANG OF IT!

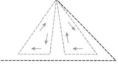

1. Quilt a 3″–4″ line parallel to the inside edge of the border. Angle back toward the top of the border, stopping about ¼″ from the edge.

2. Quilt 2 triangle-shaped wedges, both meeting at the same point.

3. Quilt a 3″–4″ horizontal line, then angle down toward the other side of the border. Stop about ¼″–½″ from the corner of the triangle you quilted in Step 1.

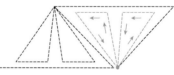

4. Fill in the space by quilting 2 triangle wedges, just as you did in Step 2.

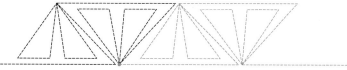

5. Continue working your way along the border, alternating the directions of the triangles and stitching wedges inside each.

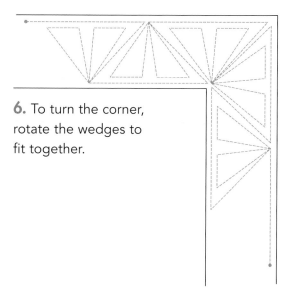

6. To turn the corner, rotate the wedges to fit together.

VARIATION

You could quilt 1 wedge instead of 2 and fill it in with a different machine-quilting design.

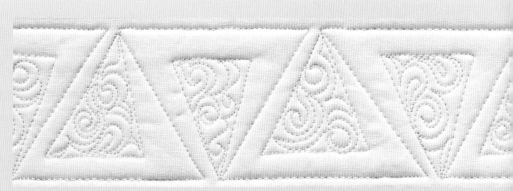

For a completely different look, stitch a single triangle inside each large triangle, and fill the smaller triangle with a curvy design.

ANGLED LINES

- -

GREAT FOR SMALL, NARROW BORDERS, THIS DESIGN IS PERFECT WHEN YOU AREN'T SURE WHAT TO DO. IT HAS SOME TRAVELING, BUT DON'T WORRY IF IT'S NOT PERFECT. THE QUILTING WILL COVER UP ANY TRAVELING MISTAKES!

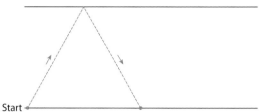

1. Quilt a diagonal line from the inside border to the outer border. Continue stitching another diagonal line back to the inside border.

note You can make the triangle as wide or as narrow as you like. It all depends on your preferences, the machine you are using, and how big you want the design to be. Sometimes you can use the piecing around the border as guide for spacing out your triangles.

2. Fill the triangle with a back-and-forth line parallel to 1 of the diagonal lines, ending at the outer edge of the border.

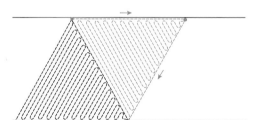

3. Travel along the edge of the border about 2″–3″, then quilt a diagonal line back to the outer point of the first triangle. Fill the new triangle with a back-and-forth line in the opposite direction as the filler in the previous triangle, ending at the tip of the triangle.

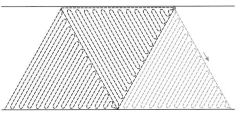

4. Continue to add triangles and fill them in, alternating the direction of the filler stitching in each triangle.

5. Continue working your way across the border and around the corner.

Align the edge of a triangle with the diagonal line of the border corner for an easy turn.

VARIATIONS

If you'd like a more open look for your borders, replace the back-and-forth filler with a few zigzag lines.

Widely spaced zigzags create more open space in the border.

Add a strong zigzag line throughout the border by leaving a little gap between the back-and-forth lines and the outer edge of each triangle.

Create a zigzag line by leaving space between the triangle edge and the filler quilting.

THIS IS WHAT I CALL A THROWBACK DESIGN. IT HAS BEEN AROUND FOR A LONG TIME AND FOR GOOD REASON. IT'S SUCH A VERSATILE DESIGN, AND I LIKE HOW THE HOOKS ON THE SWIRLS REALLY HELP FILL IN LARGE AREAS. IT'S ALSO GREAT FOR BORDERS AND SASHING.

SWIRL HOOK CHAIN

Start

1. Quilt a line that curls in toward the middle of the border. Add a "hook" by quilting a serpentine line that curves back toward the edge of the border.

2. Echo the hook back toward the swirl, stopping about ¼″ from the inside of the swirl. Continue echoing around the outside of the swirl, stopping before the border edge.

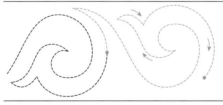

3. Quilt a new swirl facing the opposite direction from the first.

4. Add a hook and echo the swirl as in Steps 1 and 2, ending on the bottom side of the border.

5. Continue quilting swirls in alternate directions, using the hooks and echo quilting to fill in the empty spaces.

VARIATION

If you don't like the hooks, you can replace them with regular swirls in alternating directions.

Stitch regular swirls instead of hooks.

CONCLUSION

Whew! If you have made it this far into the book, I hope your head is swimming with some fun ideas for designs to use on your quilts. But no matter how you decide to quilt your next quilt top, remember this: A finished quilt is better than a perfect quilt top!

Happy quilting!

ABOUT THE AUTHOR

Angela Walters is a machine quilter and author who loves teaching others to use quilting in ways that bring out the best in their quilts. Her work has been published in numerous magazines and books. She shares tips and finished quilts on her blog, quiltingismytherapy.com, and believes that "quilting is the funnest part!"